THE KINGDOM AND PEOPLE OF KENT AD 400-1066

THE KINGDOM AND PEOPLE OF KENT AD 400-1066

THEIR HISTORY
AND ARCHAEOLOGY

STUART BROOKES AND SUE HARRINGTON

For my parents
S. B.

For Dizzie and Bill, in memorium
S. H.

First published 2010

The History Press
The Mill, Brimscombe Port
Stroud, Gloucestershire, GL5 2QG
www.thehistorypress.co.uk

British Library Cataloguing in Publication Data.
A catalogue record for this book is available from the British Library.

ISBN 978 0 7524 5694 2

Typesetting and origination by The History Press
Printed in Great Britain

CONTENTS

ACKNOWLEDGEMENTS

We would like to acknowledge the work of Vera Evison as an inspiration for the writing of this book; her excavation (1953) and publication (1987) of the cemetery of Buckland, Dover remains an outstanding contribution to our understanding of Early Anglo-Saxon Kent.

This book has benefited from the assistance given by a number of individuals and institutions that have aided our research into Anglo-Saxon Kent over the last ten years. It was first commissioned by Donald Scragg, Series Editor of a – now sadly stalled – series on the English peoples, and completed whilst we were both employed at the University College London Institute of Archaeology.

We are grateful to the following who contributed original figures and plates: Andrew Agate for the line drawings of Kentish towns; Diana Briscoe for pottery stamps; Malcolm Muir, Gabor Thomas, Steve Thoroughgood, Bexley Archaeology Group and Canterbury Archaeological Trust, Maidstone Museum and Art Gallery, and the Early Medieval Corpus of Coin Finds kindly provided photographs. Copyrighted figures are reproduced by permission of the following: Fig 11, Fig. 13 small-long brooch, Fig. 17 bracteate, Fig. 20 sword, Fig. 21 spindle-whorl, buckle, Roman suspension clip, Roman coin. All from Evison, v.i. *Dover Buckland Anglo-Saxon Cemetery* © English Heritage; Figs 7-8 © Canterbury Archaeological Trust.

Our thanks go to colleagues who contributed ideas, shared original research, and commented on drafts of the text: Gabor Thomas; Terry Burke; Gill Draper; Gustav Milne; Nathalie Cohen; John Baker; Andrew Reynolds; Inga Butefisch. Thanks as ever to Martin Welch for his long-term support of our research projects.

The final stages were overseen by Fran Cantillion of The History Press, whose help we gratefully acknowledge.

Our biggest debt of thanks goes to our families and familiars, Lis, Jerry, Evie (S.B.), Jessica, Lennie, Sidney and Ellie (S.H.) for their love and support over the long period of this book's gestation.

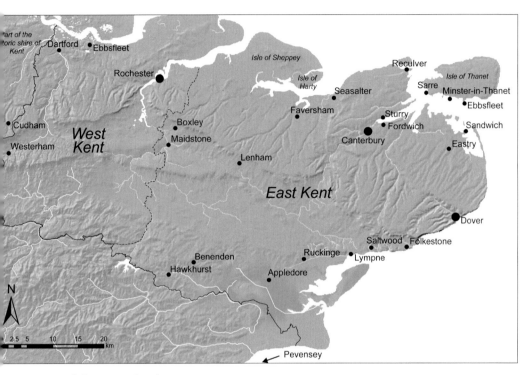

Map of places named in the text

CHAPTER 1

INTRODUCTION AND BACKGROUND

The roots of the nation we have for so many years known as England lie within the fertile soils of its earliest kingdom, the kingdom of the people of Kent (*Fig. 1*). Here, under rulers such as King Eormenric and his son Æthelberht (*c.*589–616/618), the verdant garden of England was transformed into the first recorded English kingdom. It was to provide a model that would serve all other states that followed the fall of Roman Imperial power in Britain.

Despite this long-held recognition, the birth of nations is a subject no longer popular in twenty-first century debate. Too often the nationalistic rhetoric of earlier times, trumpeting an Anglo-Saxon heritage, is now seen as cause for cringing embarrassment or outright offence. But it is a subject which offers much even to our more cynical age. Birth, by its very nature, emphasises dynamic change and flux. So, too, does it stress promise and possibility, rather than certainty and fate. Birth of nations also speaks of people and their worlds. Nations are formed through allegiances to ideas, personalities, kin, land and place. Such allegiances can be, and often are, fluid and changing.

For much of the period covered by this book, 'nations', as we might understand them, were synonymous with people. Kingship in the early medieval period was kingship over men, women and children – not land. The bonds tying Anglo-Saxon society together were the bonds between kin and their lord. Royal and dynastic authority rested on personal charisma, demonstrated ability in warfare and leadership and the control of wealth. Only over the course of the early medieval period did this authority become linked to land, to patriotism and the kingdom as a territory. In this sense, the birth of a nation is in a very real way the creation of a bounded land, demarcated in space. This book, then, describes the creation of Kent as a place and as a people.

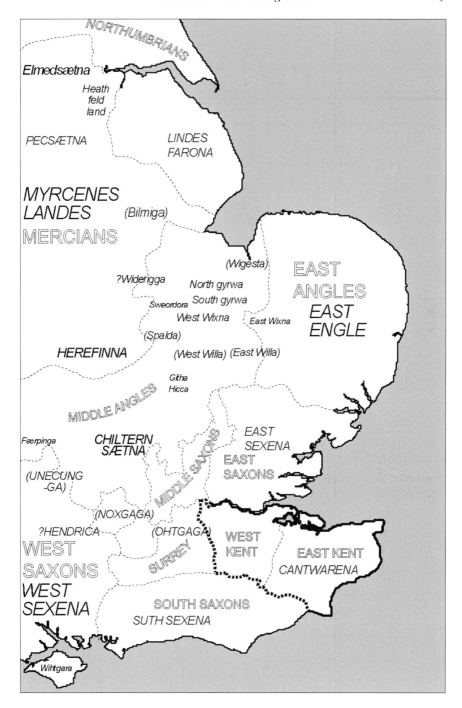

Fig. 1. Kent and the political geography of Anglo-Saxon England. In italics are the various tribal regions mentioned in the document known as the 'Tribal Hidage'; (see chapter 5) in grey, the modern names for the Anglo-Saxon kingdoms and their likely extents in the eighth century

Not that one can see this birth in isolation. 'Kent,' as the historian F.W. Maitland has observed, 'is no mountain of liberty, no remote fastness in which the remnant of an ancient race has found refuge; it is the garden of England, of all the English counties, that which is most exposed to foreign influence.' Geographically, culturally, and historically, it is the bridge to Europe, and no story of the Anglo-Saxon people of Kent can therefore be written without reference to wider social, political and economic trends both in England and abroad. But, for those very same reasons, the kingdom of Kent occupies a pivotal role in the history of early medieval England. This was where the major institutions of the medieval English state first emerged – kingship, Church, and written law – as well as the maritime capabilities that imported these ideas from Continental Europe. In looking at the evolution of the kingdom of Kent, therefore, we can see some of the ways in which these ideas took root, and flowered into the English nation.

Much of this discussion focuses on eastern Kent. The traditional division between the Men of Kent, inhabiting the lands to the east of the River Medway, and the Kentish Men, born to the west side of the same river, has a basis within the very earliest annals of Kent. This reflects the dominant kingdom of East Kent, which absorbed its smaller West Kent neighbour more than 1500 years ago. The two territories may be fossilised in the dioceses of Rochester and Canterbury. The time frame for this history of the Kentish peoples commences with the recorded departure of Roman Imperial power, *c.*AD 410, and ends with the creation, some 600 years later, of an English state under the aegis of the West Saxon kings. Kent was but a small part of this. Before looking at this uneven evolution in greater chronological detail, it is first important to clarify the sources on which our understanding of the period is based. Underpinning all discussions, however, are aspects of the physical landscape of the county, which have impacted on the development of both settlement and topography. It is to this area that we turn first.

The geology, geography and topography of Kent

The name 'Kent' appears to have a British – or pre-British – origin. It is either a Latinised British ethnic name relating to the tribal grouping, the Cantiaci, or alternatively, and perhaps preferably, it is a descriptive term meaning 'cornerland, land on the edge', referring to an incompletely defined territory comprising, at some point in its history, a large proportion of the modern south-east counties of Kent, Surrey and Sussex.

The physical topography of Kent is dominated by four geographic factors: the coastline, the river systems, the chalk downlands and the Weald. The geology underlying this structure is complex, but can generally be characterised by the dipping to the north of all of the visible layers of sediment. Processes of erosion have exposed these as outcrops, which have a directional trend more or less west–east across the county. This gives the landscape its distinctive directional grain. The variable resistance that each of these outcrops has to erosion has led to the creation of the major relief features. Taking a pass across the county (see *Fig. 2*), say from Hawkhurst in the south-west of the county to Reculver on the north coast (not in itself a practicable overland route precisely because of the intervening geology, although only a distance of some 40 miles), the geology of the first section – that of the High Weald – consists of Hastings and Wealden Clays, together with Tunbridge Wells Sands. This area contains the ironstone that supported the Wealden iron-working industries from the Roman to post-medieval periods. Above the clay vales here are also raised beds of sand.

Next we encounter the Low Weald, consisting of variable clays, which is one of the lowest-lying areas. This area is known also as the Vale of Kent. Rising above this, as we travel northeast, are the Chart Hills. These are a series of Lower Greensand beds, which are variously exposed around the rim of the Weald, narrow in parts but wider in others. This area is the source of the ubiquitous local building material, Kentish Ragstone. Between the Chart Hills and the steep scarp of the Chalk Downs, the Holmesdale is a narrow vale of Gault clay, again running around the rim of the Weald. The Chalk Downs and their dip slope to the north present the major geological feature of Kent, with the highest part at around 250m above sea level (near the Kent/Surrey border). The chalk and the dip slope are intercut by a series of dry valleys, and the chalk itself gives rise to the headwaters for a number of rivers that also flow through it. Much of the chalk is capped by Clay-with-flints. Where the Chalk Downs end at the coast, millennia of erosion have formed the high, white cliffs, most notable above Dover. A less distinctive area – generally termed as North Kent, being the belt between the Downs and the sea – is characterised by its geological diversity. Although with generally fertile soils, it includes major areas of London Clay outcrops. The Isle of Thanet exists as a chalk plateau, separated from the mainland of Kent by the Wantsum syncline, an east–west-running depression in the chalk. Edging the coast are bands of marshland, most prominent along the Thames Estuary, around the Hoo peninsular, Sheppey and at Romney.

From west to east, the chalk downs are cut by three major rivers each flowing through a broad valley, the Darenth running north into the Thames

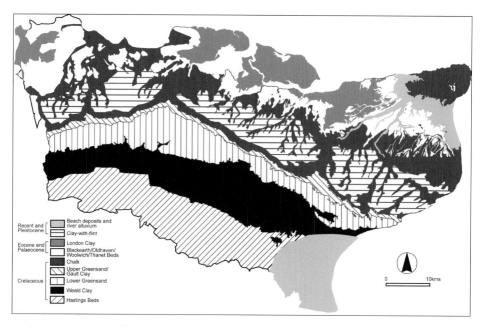

Legend:

Recent and Pleistocene	Beach deposits and river alluvium
	Clay-with-flint
Eocene and Palaeocene	London Clay
	Blackearth/Oldhaven/ Woolwich/Thanet Beds
	Chalk
Cretaceous	Upper Greensand/ Gault Clay
	Lower Greensand
	Weald Clay
	Hastings Beds

0   10kms

Fig. 2. The geology of the modern county of Kent, highlighting the southeast to northwest grain of the landscape

Estuary, the Medway, rising in the High Weald and flowing northwards into its large estuary and the Stour, running southwest to northeast and emerging via the Wantsum Channel at the east coast. The River Rother rises in the southern part of the High Weald in Sussex and flows into the English Channel to the south of Romney Marsh. Each has a network of minor tributaries rising in the Weald. A rapid overview of this transect from Hawkshurst to Reculver shows the well-wooded Wealden regions giving way to downland and then extensive areas of water, shingle beaches, estuaries, salt marshes and islands.   The soil-types present throughout the county were fundamental in determining the types of land use undertaken, and these decisions were made in a characteristically localised manner. Those areas with Wealden and London Clays would remain generally waterlogged, obviating use beyond that of pasture or woodland. The best soils, fertile with a loam or silt matrix, occur primarily in the foothills of the Downs and in the region of the Chart Hills. Indeed, the Kentish agrarian landscape has been characterised as consisting of distinctive *pays* which, as we shall identify throughout this study, have impacted on the social and economic organisation of the kingdom (*Fig. 3*). The *pays*, as identified by Alan Everitt in his volume on the evolution of Kentish settlement, are:

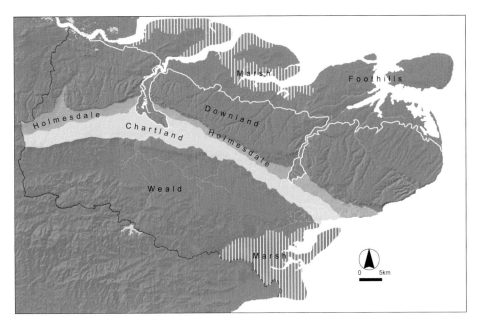

Fig. 3. The *pays* – or physiographic regions – of Kent as defined by the late Alan Everitt.
Each *pays* has distinctive landscape and environmental attributes

The Foothills of the Downs
Downland
Holmesdale
Chartland
Weald
Marshland

Everitt characterises the Foothills and the Holmesdale as the Original Lands of Kent.
These are the earliest settled zones, also known as the Old Arable Lands, reflecting
their fertile soils. The other four are identified as areas of secondary colonisation.

Kent appears now to be a relatively well-wooded county, with approximately ten per cent of its surface area so covered. The pattern of woodland
distribution and its content have changed over time, but Kent has retained
significant areas of ancient woodland, such as in the Weald, at Blean and
in dry valley areas of the North Downs in Bromley. Between the Roman
period and the recording of Domesday Book, the coverage had shrunk from
forty-five per cent to twenty-eight per cent of the overall area.

Processes of coastal erosion have had dramatic effects on the physical
geography of Kent over time, most noticeably around Sheppey, Thanet and
Romney Marsh. For the period of the fifth to tenth centuries, the Wantsum

Channel was a viable waterway, although it has long since silted over. Thanet and Sheppey extended much further out to sea, having lost up to 3km of mainland in the intervening period. The effects of coastal erosion were felt all around the coast to varying degrees. To take the example of Reculver (*Plate 1*), the present remains of the Roman fort clearly extended further to the north beyond the present cliff edge. Prior to that, however, there was a settlement approximately two kilometres further still to the north that was lost in Roman times, such was the pace of coastal change. The movement of eroded sediment assisted in the formation of extensive coastal marshes that would eventually be reclaimed for agricultural land by inning. Despite these changes, Kent retained a good supply of coastal inlets, estuaries and navigable rivers throughout, though the varying build-ups of shingle and sediment at times restricted the size of vessel that could access them. The climatic conditions during the era of the Kentish kingdom provide evidence of phases of warmer and cooler episodes, with climatic instability in the sixth and ninth centuries producing more storms and increased rainfall.

The archaeological sources

The framework established by the documentary sources discussed below has informed many of the interpretations made from the archaeological evidence. The relationship between 'archaeology' (based on the physical remains of the past) and 'history' (based on events recorded in written sources) of an historic and proto-historic period such as this, remains a live and contested issue. Although some scholars perceive one source as more valuable than the other, it is generally accepted that each has a different set of attributes to bring to the research table. Whatever the approach, the subjects of past society and economy have proved amongst the most fruitful for investigation. For archaeologists, a particularly rich source of evidence – which is overwhelmingly prevalent in the archaeological record of southern England – is that of cemeteries. Indeed, so rich is funerary archaeology in Kent that the region figures prominently in all discussions of Anglo-Saxon England. A long history of archaeological interventions – that is, the great wealth of material and the large numbers of Anglo-Saxon burials found, especially in eastern Kent – have provided the source material for many of the studies on artefacts and mortuary behaviour. Yet it can be argued that Kentish archaeology has become divorced from that of other areas of Anglo-Saxon England and, in some senses, has become a place apart – a special place wherein the processes of social, economic and cultural development identified elsewhere do not, apparently, manifest themselves in the same way.

The excavation history of the early Anglo-Saxon Kent cemeteries has been variously documented, mainly in the annals of *Archaeologia Cantiana*, and has been extensively discussed elsewhere. Here, the phases of excavation can be briefly summarised. The earliest excavations of Anglo-Saxon graves in Kent are attested from the seventeenth century and surviving records detailing finds at Reculver in 1700, Crundale in 1703 and Greenwich in 1714 suggest widespread antiquarian interest in the – then still visible – mortuary structures, such as burial mounds, throughout the early eighteenth century (*Fig. 4*). Antiquarian investigations were followed by academic and public sector involvement to the point where, currently, professional archaeological contractors and field units are the most active practitioners.

Individual antiquarians, such as the Reverend Bryan Faussett, James Douglas, John Brent, Cecil Brent, George Payne and Charles Roach Smith, dominated archaeological research in Kent. They keenly investigated sites prominent in the landscape, including extensive barrow cemeteries often located on land belonging to the local aristocracy. In so doing, they developed their own excavation techniques, employing probing rods to find potential deposits and agricultural labour for excavation work. The great misfortune is that these rudimentary archaeological techniques effectively erased the burial mounds from the landscape.

The antiquarians' key finds might be reported to their peers at the Society of Antiquaries of London and, later, to the Royal Archaeological Institute and the British Archaeological Association. In addition, they recovered materials through purchase finds literally thrown up by navigation engineers during the construction of railways in Kent – doing so before the finds could be sold off to less reputable prospective buyers. Other earth-moving activities, such as gravel extraction and chalk quarrying, similarly exposed hitherto-unknown burial sites. In addition to excavations, records of further finds by that invaluable chronicler of Kent, Edward Hasted (1732–1812), and by the collector, William Boys (1792), present us with a reasonably detailed picture of the Anglo-Saxon mortuary landscape as it was known in the eighteenth century.

Amongst the earliest-published cemetery sites are a large number identified and excavated by the Revd Bryan Faussett between 1760 and 1773. Faussett recorded the individual graves to a standard that was well in advance of his time, and his recording of these saw his notes posthumously published in the *Inventorium Sepulchrale* (1856). Unfortunately, the collection itself had a more turbulent history. Turned down for acquisition by the British Museum, it was purchased by Joseph Mayer (1803–86) and transferred to Liverpool in

BARFRISTON DOWN, 1854.

Fig. 4. A nineteenth-century view across Barfriston Down. The antiquarian Revd Bryan Faussett and his team of navvies dug through most of the burial mounds here in the eighteenth century

the nineteenth century. The carefully detailed contextual information for the artefacts recorded by Faussett, regarding site and grave number, was rendered less than useful due to the disarticulation of most grave-good assemblages. Although some artefacts can be re-identified via the published illustrations, most of the 'mundane' material cannot be placed in a grave, or indeed, in most cases, even into the correct cemetery context. Additionally, some subsequent dispersal and the Second World War bombing of Liverpool City Museum, which saw the material from the extensive Ozengell cemetery lost, has further denuded the collection. (Although, as we shall see, the situation has not proved to be wholly irretrievable.)

Unfortunately, the Faussett Collection was not alone in its fate. The material excavated by John Brent at Sarre in 1863 perhaps most usefully illustrates the scale of the 'collection traumas' of the period. This cemetery was extensively investigated and published in some detail in *Archaeologia Cantiana*, with unusual care being taken to record individual grave assemblages, their position *in situ* and other factors affecting their deposition. Although a cemetery plan was produced, no individual grave plans exist, nor was any mention made of grave structures. Custodianship of the material fell to a number of institutions, including the British Museum, Maidstone Museum, Cambridge University and the Ashmolean, Rochester and Canterbury museums. (The 1990 material from Sarre is located in the Trust for Thanet Archaeology headquarters, near Broadstairs.) Subsequent handling and archiving has, however, again managed to disassociate most of the artefacts from their original grave contexts. In addition, much of the Sarre material housed in Maidstone Museum has also become interspersed with artefacts from Bifrons, excavated by T.G. Godfrey-Faussett in 1867. This has made the reassignment of material, even to the correct cemetery, a difficult task.

Perhaps more serious is the loss of the material from King's Field, Faversham. Combined railway construction and brick-earth digging all but destroyed the clearly exceptional Anglo-Saxon cemetery between 1858 and 1874. Despite significant antiquarian interest in the site, only a few graves were recorded (by John Brent in 1874), and the large body of material remaining from the cemetery today is both of uncertain contexts and diffused across a number of collections. Any examination of the extant material, particularly that held by the British Museum, illustrates the exceptional quality and range of high-status objects, whose constituent materials include gold, amber and amethysts. These are perhaps only a fraction of what might have been retrieved in different circumstances.

The twentieth century saw the advent of more concerted efforts to recover whole cemeteries intact, using modern excavation methods. This phase relied on the enthusiasm of experienced amateurs and groups, such as local and county archaeological societies (*Fig. 5*), working together with academic specialists from within the relatively new discipline of Anglo-Saxon archaeology, most notably Vera Evison and Sonia Chadwick Hawkes. The involvement of national bodies such as the British Museum and the Ministry of Public Buildings and Works was particularly important to these undertakings. The situation, however, demanded rapid reaction to the imminent destruction of valuable material, rather than being primarily driven by a clearly defined research agenda and plan of campaign. The notable exception was the excavation at Finglesham in the 1960s and 1970s, which aimed at the near total investigation of a whole cemetery. The majority of the work carried out in this period was sparsely funded and reliant on the wherewithal of the site director to bring knowledge of the cemeteries into the public domain and to secure the future of the site archive. The increased pace of building and infrastructural development throughout the region had sparked a number of what were essentially rescue excavations during the 1950s and 1960s, often in difficult circumstances.

The sites excavated by Vera Evison have been fully published, and much of the basic dating, chronology and overall patterning for the early Anglo-Saxon period in use today is a direct result of this careful and well-researched work, providing an exemplary resource for the next generation of researchers

Fig. 5. The excavation at Horton Kirby, Riseley in 1938, carried out by the Dartford District Archaeology Group

into the Anglo-Saxon settlement. By contrast, the piecemeal publication of some early cemeteries and almost all of those excavated either fully or partially since 1970 has in many ways hampered the research agenda for early Anglo-Saxon Kent. The publication of Mill Hill Deal I by Keith Parfitt & Birte Brugmann in 1997 provides the most important recent source (the publication of the second excavation at Buckland, Dover still pending). It is unfortunate, from the point of view of wishing to compare it with other sites, that Mill Hill Deal was only in use during the sixth century – we still await the advent of a major seventh-century cemetery site excavated to modern archaeological standards. The final publication of the archives of Sonia Chadwick Hawkes, including the excavation at Finglesham and her catalogue of Bifrons, has filled in some of the missing pieces of the jigsaw.

Professional archaeological contractors are a more recent phenomenon, working to specific briefs and funded by developers in the wake of PPG 16 (Planning Policy Guidance, note 16). Due to the United Kingdom's closer political and economic links with mainland Europe in the last forty years,

Kent has been the location for both publicly and privately funded development on a major scale. This has resulted in an increased pace of archaeological work, as these projects, such as the infrastructure around the Channel Tunnel and the location of retail outlets on greenfield sites, have impacted on the landscape. New sites discovered include cemeteries at Saltwood and Cuxton on the line of the Channel Tunnel Rail Link. The additional benefit of this latest phase of work has been the uncovering of small areas of early Anglo-Saxon settlement sites, which complement the cemetery evidence. Kent is fortunate in having locally-based excavators, each of which has contributed to the recovery of material. Mention must be made here of the professional contractors West Kent Archaeological Rescue Unit, Canterbury Archaeological Trust and the Trust for Thanet Archaeology. But mention too must be made of the local amateur societies, many of which have tackled the excavation of a few burials or a whole cemetery throughout their histories, for example Dartford Archaeology Group, Orpington and District Archaeological Society, Bexley Archaeological group and the Dover group (*Plate 2*).

The focus of attention by antiquarians and academics on the range of jewelled brooches particularly associated with early Anglo-Saxon East Kent had been at the expense of research into the more mundane items within the grave good assemblages, from which the brooches may then have become disassociated. In addition, the sheer volume of ironwork deposited in the early Anglo-Saxon period has brought problems for conservation and storage, particularly for material excavated before the modern era. Only modern excavations have sought to exploit the full range of potential data from these sites, such as organics, demography and skeletal analysis, textiles and metallurgy. Significant and very welcome advances in recording and dissemination have been made in recent years, mainly through the use of digital technology. The reader is referred to the list of relevant websites in the Further Reading section.

The foregoing section has concentrated mainly on the excavation record of early Anglo-Saxon cemeteries for the overriding reason that these dominate the archaeological landscape. Yet, for the whole period of the Anglo-Saxon kingdom to our end point in the eleventh century, there is also a wealth of other material available. Whilst the earliest timber buildings of the majority of the settlement sites have not survived, we do have the standing buildings of the Saxon shore forts in use during the early part of our period, major ecclesiastical sites, together with early church foundations and minsters, although some can only be inferred from documentary sources. Perhaps most useful

are the networks of roads, trackways and droving routes that framed activity throughout the landscape – whilst many of these may be prehistoric and
Roman in origin, many of the hollow ways and earthworks are the rem-
nants of Anglo-Saxon landscape divisions. The structure of parish boundaries
might also fall within this category.

At the time of writing, the range of archaeological resources available from
Kent as a whole includes 657 sites, comprising: 36 early church foundations;
124 cemeteries; 174 separate coin finds; 9 crop marks; 60 settlements; 83 isolated burials and 173 find spots, mainly of metal objects. These cemeteries
and burials contained approximately 3,500 individuals, and we have records
of approximately 12,000 objects, mainly deposited as grave goods but also
including casual losses. Nevertheless, this is not an exhaustive list, derived
as it is from ASKED (the Anglo-Saxon Kent Electronic Database), a research
tool built collaboratively by the authors, detailing all known sites up to 2001.
The discovery of new sites continues and now must be added over 400 find
spot locations of metalwork generated by the Portable Antiquities Scheme,
reported since 2001.

The historical sources

The comparatively large numbers of historical records for Anglo-Saxon Kent,
some of which are the earliest known sources for the period as a whole, have
ensured that the kingdom has been featured prominently in over-arching
explanations and models of Anglo-Saxon state formation – the understanding of which is a key research issue for historians and archaeologists alike.
This was as true in the Venerable Bede's day as it is in modern times. Bede's
emphasis on the centrality to English history of the Augustinian mission to
Kent in AD 597 and the importance Kentish sources played in providing the
information for his narrative history mean that this kingdom features prominently throughout his *Historia Ecclesiastica* (*HE*).

The story of Hengest and Horsa's arrival in three boats at Ebbsfleet in AD
449 and the call for 'more' Anglian, Saxon and Jutish mercenaries from their
homelands to settle in this territory has been retold on numerous occasions,
and the reader is referred to the Further Reading section at the end of the
book for discussions of this issue. The Kentish origin myth is preserved in
the *HE* as well as the *Historia Brittonum* (*HB*) and the *Anglo-Saxon Chronicle*
(*ASC*), and additional fragments of the royal genealogy and annals are found
in the 'Anglian Collection' and other continental manuscripts. To these can be
added further sources, in the form of the law codes of Æthelberht, Hlothhere

and Eadric, and of Wihtred (see Appendices and *Plate 3*), as well as contemporary diplomas and charters, which provide important evidence closer in date to actual events – as indeed does Gregory of Tours' *Historiae Francorum* (*HF*) and copies of papal letters relating to the progress of the Gregorian mission. It must be reiterated that these foundation events were recorded at some time later than what was clearly the migration of people into Kent, on whatever scale, in the wake of the fragmentation of Roman Imperial power in Britain in the early fifth century (discussed in chapter 2 on the Sub-Roman province). Latterly, researchers have had access to a significant and insightful additional source of document-based information, that of place names, many of which appear to chart the naming anew of settlement in the landscape by people who spoke a Germanic – rather than Brittonic – language.

Bede identifies the first wave of settlers as being the aforementioned warriors, invited to come and protect the eastern part of the island of Britain in return for land grants so that they could settle amongst the native Britons. A second and larger wave followed shortly afterwards, also receiving land grants, and these newcomers are named as Saxons, Angles and Jutes. For many, Kent is synonymous with the 'Jutish Kingdom', settled by people from Jutland (the mainland part of modern-day Denmark), and it is from them that the people of Kent are traditionally descended.

What might we conjecture about the make-up of these two waves of migrant settlers? Were the first incomers into Kent single-sex groups of men, perhaps tied by kinship or at least with a common tribal allegiance, who then settled and intermarried with Romano-British local women? Was the second wave different in that they were mixed sex groups of extended families, which included women and children? Indeed, how many could there have been to make the profound impact indicated by the documentary sources? Evidently, these people maintained links with their north European homelands, which might have facilitated subsequent migration events.

However, Bede tells us that 'it was not long before such hordes of these alien people vied together to crowd into the island that the natives who had invited them began to live in terror'. Eventually, the 'heathen conquerors' devastated the island from east to west, with butchery or slavery the only outcomes for the 'wretched survivors'. Yet the total depopulation of Kent, with its extensive network of ports, towns and good farmland, and complete population replacement is difficult to imagine, even within this harrowing account, and many modern authors assume that some process of acculturation took place, whereby indigenous and immigrant communities assimilated. Did elements of the local population survive to become people of Kent themselves?

According to the Kentish origin myth, the kingdom was subsequently consolidated by Hengest's son Œris Oisc (AD 488–?512), the ancestral figurehead of the Kentish royal genealogy. The Oiscingas' rule at this time is likely to have been restricted to territories to the east of the Medway. Barbara Yorke has effectively argued that the foundation of the two bishoprics of Kent shortly after conversion, at Canterbury (AD 597) and Rochester (AD 604), crystallised both a cultural and political division of the kingdom into its eastern and western parts (discussed in chapter 3 on the formation of Anglo-Saxon communities). Documentary evidence that later administration was initially through dual kings and then *ealdormen*, has hinted at the existence of a primary East Kent kingdom that annexed the province to the west from more ethnically 'Saxon' *gens* during the sixth century.

The formation of the Kentish kingdom during this period might be linked to expansionist policies in contemporary Francia, suggesting that Kent developed as a peripheral state as a result of the creation of a new northern economic area, tied to the Merovingian Frankish aristocracy. However, there are only a few direct allusions regarding Frankish policy to the north of Francia in the writings of the main chroniclers of the time – Gregory of Tours, Ventatius Fortunatus, Fredegar and Procopius – so that the documentary evidence for the sixth and seventh centuries provides only fragmentary insights into the political reality of the period, and moreover reflects very much a Frankish perspective on contemporary events. Nevertheless, Kent certainly profited from Continental contacts at this time: archaeology confirms the presence in eastern Kent of numerous objects of gold, silver and precious jewels, deriving from Francia, the Low Countries, Scandinavia and beyond. But were these the result of trade, migration, diplomacy, or piracy? Chapter 3 examines the evidence to assess both the external influences on Kent and the character and form of Kentish society in the sixth century.

The kingdom of Kent passes from Dark Age obscurity to historical reality with the coming to power of Eormenric (?–*c*.AD 589) and his son Æthelberht (*c*.AD 589–616/8), both of whom are mentioned in Gregory of Tours' narrative history (*HF*). It is under these rulers that the kingdom first appears to take on its developed form, with membership to the royal house captured in a written genealogy, and centralised authority and laws of the realm enshrined in codes (discussed in chapter 4 on Æthelbehrt's Kent). Æthelbehrt is immortalised by Bede for being the first Christian ruler of Kent, and for facilitating the conversion of the English, but he may also have held, at least temporarily, wide-ranging authority over many of the other tribes of eastern and southern England. More locally, his reign is of further significance, as it was in the decades either side of AD 600 that a 'Kentish' people firmly aligned with the royal house.

More English written sources exist from the seventh to ninth centuries – known as the Middle Anglo-Saxon period (AD 650–850) – from which to assess the state of Kentish affairs. Notable amongst these sources is Bede's *HE* itself, but also a document known as the *Tribal Hidage* and the earliest charters (discussed in chapter 5). These sources document Kent's changing fortunes following Æthelbehrt's death. Certainly none of his descendents were again to command his level of political authority as powerful leaders emerged amongst the Angles, West Saxons and Mercians. Encouraged by dynastic tensions within Kent during the seventh century, these kings assumed greater political, military and economic power, gradually wresting away Kentish power and establishing independent links with the Continent. Kentish control of London appears already to have come under threat during the reign of Eadbald (AD 616–640), and by the mid-seventh century, dominions in Surrey had passed to Mercia. In AD 685, Jutish territories on the Isle of Wight fell to Caedwalla of Wessex, as did, briefly, Kent itself in the following year. Between King Wihtred's submission to Ine of Wessex in AD 694 and the kingdom's final incorporation by the West Saxons in AD 825, Kent retained only fitful independence from Mercian and West Saxon rule.

Despite the uncertainties of secular politics, the consolidation of the ecclesiastical power, wealth and ideology, and the growth in towns and industry, provided the parameters for social stability in the centuries after the Augustinian Mission. The Viking raids from AD 830, by contrast, transformed the pattern of tenure (discussed in chapter 6 on Later Anglo-Saxon Kent, AD 850–1066). By 900, the devastation of monastic life had led to an extensive secularisation of Church lands as approximately a fifth of the taxable lands passed to the West Saxon kings, although some of these estates eventually passed back into Church hands (e.g. Reculver and Lyminge, granted to Christchurch in AD 949 and 964 respectively, and Minster-in-Thanet to St Augustine's Canterbury, in AD 964). The changes in land tenure during the latter half of the ninth century, and the economic changes in the landscape resulting from this period of turmoil, effectively ensured that the situation in Kent in the period from then until the Norman Conquest of AD 1066 was radically different. Instead of existing as a separate state, Kent formed merely a province of a larger kingdom of England: economically, militarily, and legally tied to the rest of the nation.

CHAPTER 2

FIFTH-CENTURY KENT: A SUB-ROMAN PROVINCE?

Introduction

Momentous changes to the economic, social and political structures of the area we now know as Kent took place in the fifth century AD. But Sonia Chadwick Hawkes has realistically characterised the period, for researchers, as being reduced to 'the status of a kind of no-man's-land between the secure entrenchments of known Roman and unambiguous Saxon' (1961; 1). Clearly the fourth-century Roman cultural landscape was different from that of the Anglo-Saxon sixth century, but how much can we identify of the changes that took place? To pursue this question, the chapter is divided into three sections: Late Roman Kent; The Migration; and The Settlement.

Traditional views, inspired by readings of Bede, perceive the fifth century as the time when the Germans came to Britain. However, the very notion of a mass migration by people from Northern Europe is challenged by arguments stressing concepts of acculturation, or the adoption of a new material culture by the surviving Sub-Roman population. The position adopted here, though, is that such radical changes cannot be explained easily by an either/or approach. The processes of early state formation, from a Sub-Roman province to the earliest attested English kingdom, are complex. The weight of archaeological evidence and that from literary sources favours migrations into Kent as the prime factor within a very volatile context, although acculturation arguments may well be more compelling in other regions of England, particularly in the Upper Thames Valley.

Late Roman Kent

The ending of Roman influence in Britain is generally taken to be concurrent with the departure of the Roman legions by AD 407 to deal with incursions across the frontiers of the Empire elsewhere, and Emperor Honorius' message in AD 410 that henceforth the Britons should look to their own defence. It can be argued that this historical event has now placed an unwieldy and unhelpful division between Roman and Anglo-Saxon studies. But, if we are to understand anything of the *Adventus Saxonium* (the coming of the Saxons), we need to be aware of those other elements of the waning Roman culture before this point that affected the events of the fifth century in Kent. Can we identify evidence of a hiatus – a complete break with the Roman past – or can we find strands of continuity?

Roman Britain of the late third and fourth centuries was subject to persistent piratical raiding by Franks, Saxons, Picts and Scots. As the closest point of contact with mainland Europe and the shortest sea crossing, Kent must have been particularly susceptible to attack. In the fifth century Sidonius Apollinarius regarded both the Franks and Saxons as maritime peoples. Certainly Saxon piracy was a common feature in the North Sea until well into the sixth century, and the *Litus Saxonicum* (the 'Saxon Shore'), mentioned in the *Notitia Dignitatum*, implies that Saxons were the most prominent group of Germanic seafarers to trouble the coast of late Roman Britain. From the mid-third century onwards, the main response by the Romans to these incursions had been the building of a series of substantial military and naval bases around the coast – the Saxon shore forts (*Fig. 6*). The question remains unresolved however, as to whether the term 'Saxon Shore' refers to 'the coast subject to attack by Saxons' or 'the coast settled by Saxons'. In any event, the former at least must hold true. The forts were placed from Brancaster (*Branodunum*) near the Wash to Portchester (*Portus Adurni*) in Hampshire and possibly Carisbrooke on the Isle of Wight. Kent had a concentration of four strategically placed forts at Reculver (*Regulbium*), Richborough (*Rutupiae*, Plate 4), Dover (*Dubris*) and Lympne (*Lemanis*), with the somewhat isolated fort at Pevensey (*Anderita*) in East Sussex, with its back to the vast tracts of woodland know known as the Weald, next in the sequence.

The *Notitia Dignitatum* lists those regular detachments of the Roman army manning the forts in the late fourth century, but it is generally accepted that Germanic mercenaries from northern Gaul would have reinforced these troops. Indeed, given that Lympne was probably abandoned in the mid-fourth century and its detachment transferred to Pevensey, the region between *Anderita* and *Rutupiae* may well have been the focus for the

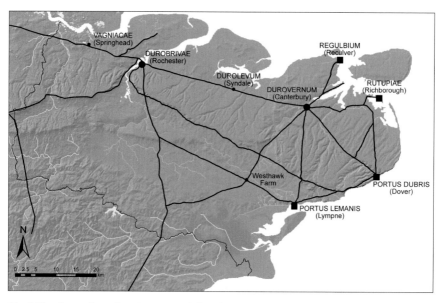

Fig. 6. The Saxon shore forts in Kent and their linking Roman roads and major trackways

settlement of *foederati*. Distinctions must be outlined here for the terms *foed-erati* and *laeti*, both of which relate to the well-used Roman strategy wherein Germanic people were settled with grants of land in exchange for military service just within the border of the Empire, in order to protect the frontier from incursions by other Germanic peoples. *Foederati* were tribal groups that had originally arrived through conquest, but whose tenure of the land was confirmed by a treaty or *foedus* in return for military duties. They retained their own tribal identity, although this would have become blurred over time, particularly if their chieftains attained high rank within the Roman army. *Laeti*, on the other hand, were groups of German people installed purposely by the Romans in under-populated areas as farming settlers, but whose men-folk also owed military duties. Their social status was thus semi-free and tied to the land.

Excavations at Richborough have shown that it was one of the last places to have been held in any military strength and is the source of numerous examples of Late Roman military metalwork, such as weapons, ornaments, buckles and strap ends. Similar finds at Lullingstone, Snodland and Milton near Sittingbourne suggest that *foederati* may have been stationed further inland as well. However, such *foederati* may well have become culturally assimilated, using prevalent Romanised forms of everyday goods and burial practices – they are hard to distinguish in the archaeological record of the fourth century – and may appear to us just as any other Romanised population, whatever their ethnic origins. Recurring finds of fifth-century forms of Roman military metalwork, used in Britain but probably manufactured in the area around the Rhineland, are changing our view of the distribution of these mercenary settlers. Such finds are mainly produced by metal detectorists working throughout Kent and highlight the cumulative value of recordings with the Portable Antiquities Scheme since its inception in 1997.

In any event, if the situation regarding the military defence of Britain at the end of the fourth century was in a parlous state, that of the civilian administration was no better. Well-founded judgements of the insecurity of the situation had prompted the upper classes to move away from their countryside villa estates to the fortified towns. Yet, we do have evidence of continued habitation activity at the villa sites at Lullingstone and Darenth in West Kent in the first quarter of the fifth century, although at a much reduced scale. The Britons repulsed a critical Saxon invasion in AD 408, but a probable peasant revolt thereafter resulted in the expulsion of the remaining civil administrators, perhaps finally throwing off the yoke of Roman imperialism. The supply of goods to the army had been a major element of the economy and once that had been removed so too went the pressure on the peasantry to produce surpluses for the market, such as foodstuffs and cloth, and to pay taxes. They may well have resisted physically such impositions. The economy of Roman Kent had probably already ground to a halt, as the importation of coinage had been drastically reduced during the fourth century. Nevertheless, localised administrations must have continued to some degree, perhaps organised by the landowning aristocracy. As Alec Detsicas has characterised the situation:

> It can only be conjectured that sub-Roman Britain fragmented into regional factions of usurpers vying with each other for ascendancy until, out of the resulting disorganisation, there emerged, perhaps about 425, the *superbus tyrannus* figure of Vortigern.

But, to back track a little from this historically attested figure, we know that there were few remaining cultural elements in the late fourth century that can identify for us in the archaeological record a continuation of the Roman lifestyle, implying with good justification that there was a widespread cultural collapse in the fourth century. We have few coins in circulation (and probably as bullion rather than within a money-based economy), the pottery industries had ceased to produce on a commercial scale and the Wealden iron industry was in abeyance. Urban life appears to have come to an end, to be covered in the layer of organic matter known as 'Dark Earth'.

This might appear to indicate that there was wholesale depopulation throughout Roman Britain. However, small rural sites, the native farmsteads that were the homes of the Romano-British peasantry, may have continued in use, but at a subsistence level producing only enough for their own needs or for a very local exchange of goods and services – it is this type of site that is most difficult to detect archaeologically and unsurprisingly we have scant evidence for such sites.

The evidence from the towns is variable. Canterbury, at the centre of the strategically important road network linking the coastal forts with London (*Fig. 6*), remained important to the end, although it, in common with many other towns, shows evidence of declining population and reduced activity from the late third century onwards. Extensive archaeological excavations within the Roman walled area of the town have shown that stone repair work was still being carried out in the late fourth century, with timber structures more in evidence, possibly extending into the early fifth. Work by Canterbury Archaeological Trust at the Ridingate (*Fig. 7*) has shown that, although it was partially closed to restrict access to the walled city, a metal-working shop may have been set up there, possibly in use in the early fifth century. In addition, we have the somewhat enigmatic evidence of a multiple burial at Stour Street, which has also been dated to the early fifth century (*Fig. 8*).

Fig. 7. A reconstruction drawing of the Ridingate, Canterbury, *c.*AD 300, based on archaeological excavation. Image drawn by John Atherton Bowen, courtesy of Canterbury Archaeological Trust

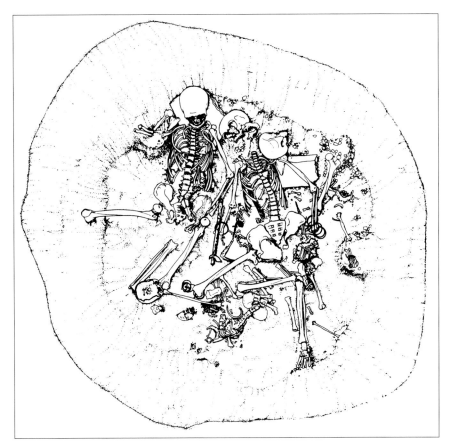

Fig. 8. The Stour Street group burial. Image courtesy of Canterbury Archaeological Trust Ltd

Consisting of a family group of male and female adults with two children and the family dog, they had been placed in a grass-lined pit within the Roman temple precinct. Although the females had Roman ornaments, they also had glass beads imported from Germanic areas of northern Europe – bead types that re-occur in pagan burials of the sixth century in Kent.

Roman Rochester, at a crucial bridging point for Watling Street over the Medway, shows, at present, no evidence that it was occupied after the early fifth century, although it has not been subject to large-scale excavations that might identify ephemeral traces of ongoing activity (*Plate 5*). Roman Dover, despite having had a major role as the main port of entry to Britain, was to all intents and purposes abandoned by the end of the fourth century, although as a location and with its remaining Roman infrastructure it was, as we shall see, to emerge in the Anglo-Saxon era as a key place for trade and exchange. It is probable that, to a limited extent, the major road network remained viable, as it appears as an important structuring element of early Anglo-Saxon landscape patterns, although the minor networks linking farmsteads with small towns and villas perhaps fell out of use. The northern section of the London to Lewes Roman road, crossing the North Downs via Addington and Cudham, is a case in point, in that it attains significance in the early seventh century as part of the western edge of the Christian diocese of Rochester and to the present day forms a section of the boundary between Kent and Surrey (*Plate 6*).

Did Roman Christianity survive in Kent? Clearly in the fifth century, it did survive in the Celtic West of Britain, but the evidence for Kent is shadowy. The first question is how far in any case this religion had permeated through Romano-British society. It might be suggested that it was mainly the religion of the urban classes and that pre-Roman Celtic type cults may have survived in rural areas. We have the evidence of a hexagonal masonry font at Richborough, the possible continued use of a chapel at Lullingstone and the rebuild of an octagonal baptismal bath at Bax Farm, near Teynham, together with various contemporary artefacts displaying the *chi-rho* monogram, all dateable to the early fifth century, to suggest a few last bastions of Christianity in Roman Kent, but beyond these scattered outposts, nothing.

The migration

This period has been called the Dark Ages within British scholarship, due to the relative absence of contemporary documentary sources, the perception of it as barbarous and pagan and without the light of Christianity. Our continental counterparts, however, study the period known as the 'Völkerwandrungszeit', the time of the movement of people, wherein entire tribes, or groups with a common ethnicity, journeyed across Europe from the north towards the south and from the east towards the west (*Fig. 9*). These journeys took place over several centuries, between the fourth and the seventh, and whilst the reasons for these titanic shifts in population were various, we can point to several potentially key factors, many of which are familiar within the context of modern European phases of migration. Amongst these are: land hungers, where the current land holding was insufficient to support the (expanding) population forcing people to look elsewhere for habitation; pressure from other migrating groups forcing onward movement, perhaps into already settled areas elsewhere; the breaching of the Roman frontiers in northern Europe attracting successive settlement within its former boundaries; and climate change. This last issue manifested itself in northern Europe with wetter and warmer conditions from the early fifth century onwards,

Fig. 9. 'The Arrival of the First Ancestors of Englishmen out of Germany into Britain', from *A Restitution of Decayed Intelligence* by Richard Verstegan (1605)

reaching a climax perhaps in the late fifth century, but continuing its effects until *c.*AD 800. Studies have identified a melting of the Arctic ice cap, caused by a rise in sea temperature. The net effect for the coastal regions of the North Sea would have been a rise in sea level, altering the shape of the coastline and probably rendering the lowest lying areas uninhabitable.

Both the historical and the archaeological evidence attest to the fact of migration by tribal peoples into Britain and the documentary sources from Anglo-Saxon England give us a narrative that is worth repeating in full. But writing as archaeologists, one does not expect this narrative to be fully replicated in the archaeological record, nor indeed should the archaeological record be coerced into reflecting specific historic events. The interplay between documented events and sites and objects cannot necessarily be used to confirm or refute assertions about the Anglo-Saxon settlement. So, let us deal first with what the documents actually record about the migration into Kent, within the wider context of the arrival of people from northern Europe along the eastern and southern seaboard of Britain, before considering the developing body of archaeological evidence. The major sources that will be referred to here are the *Anglo-Saxon Chronicle* (*ASC*) and the Venerable Bede's 'A History of the English Church and People' (*HE*). Both documents were written at a considerable temporal remove from the events of the fifth century, relying on oral histories, perhaps distorted by the very different culture and politics of mid and late Anglo-Saxon England. There are strong elements of the creation of 'origin myths', essentially using the past to justify the present. The reader is referred to the Further Reading section for more discussions of these issues. Nevertheless, whatever reservations one might have about these sources, particularly in their dating schema and their naming of key individuals, they do outline a complex and swiftly changing sequence of events that may have occurred in the fifth century.

There are several surviving manuscripts of the *ASC*, with slight variations (that transcribed here is mainly from the Canterbury Manuscript, with our additional comments in square brackets), which tell us that in AD 418: 'Here the Romans assembled all the gold-hoards which were in Britain and hid some in the earth so that no one afterwards could find them, and took some with them into Gaul', suggesting an exodus of the Roman aristocracy and their wealth from Britain, perhaps via Richborough. In AD 443:

> Here the Britons sent to Rome and asked them for help against the Picts, but they had none there because they were campaigning against Attila, King of the Huns; and then they sent to the Angles and made the same request to the princes of the Angle race.

In AD 449:

> Hengest and Horsa, invited by Vortigern, king of the Britons, sought out Britain in the landing-place which is named Ebba's Creek, at first to help the Britons, but later they fought against them. The king ordered them to fight against the Picts, and they did so and had victory wheresoever they came. Then they sent to Angeln and ordered them to send more help, and told them of the worthlessness of the Britons and the excellence of the land. They then sent them more help. These men came from three tribes of Germany: from the Old Saxons, from the Angles, from the Jutes. From the Jutes came the Cantware and the Wihtware – that is the tribe that now lives on Wight – and that race in Wessex which they still call the Jutes. From the Old Saxons came the East Saxons and South Saxons and West Saxons. From Angeln, which has stood waste ever since between the Jutes and the Saxons, came the East Angles, Middle Angles, Mercians, and all the Northumbrians.

Ebba's Creek is the place now known as Ebbsfleet, near Sandwich, located at the entrance to the Wantsum Channel, at that time a navigable waterway between the Isle of Thanet and the mainland, opposite the Roman fort at Richborough. Angeln is the neck of land between mainland Germany and that part of Denmark known as Jutland.

In AD 455, the *ASC* reports that:

> Here Hengist and Horsa fought against Vortigern the king in the place which is called Aylesford [a fording place of the River Medway, a site chosen for engagement rather than the possibly defended bridge further upstream at Rochester], and his brother Horsa was killed. And after that Hengest, and Æsc his son, succeeded to the kingdom.

And in AD 456:

> Here Hengest and Æsc fought against the Britons at a place which is called Crayford [the last major river crossing – of the Darenth – on the approach to London], and there killed 4 troops [variously recorded as 4000 troops and 4 troops of Britons]; and the Britons then abandoned the land of Kent and in great terror fled to the stronghold of London.

Finally, in AD 465, it reports:

> Here Hengest and Æsc fought against the Welsh [i.e. the British] near Wipped's Creek [an as yet unidentified place, although probably not in Kent] …

The chronicle continues with accounts of other successful conquests in southern Britain, with the very conspicuous element of other pairs of named heroic warriors, Ælle and Cissa, Cerdic and Cynric and Stuf and Wihtgar, hinting that this style of pairing was a conceit of oral history and bardic constructs rather than a factual record.

Whilst the *ASC* provides us with a record of conflict, duplicity and conquest by an incoming warrior elite, more tactically astute in overcoming the poorly led and prone to flight British, the account of the Venerable Bede covering the events of the fifth century hints at a more nuanced process of settlement. Bede of necessity concentrates on the narrative elements culminating in the conversion of various Anglo-Saxon kings, developing from the pivotal arrival of the Augustinian Mission into Kent in AD 597. In the period of the late fourth to early fifth centuries he narrates that famine was prevalent in Britain prompting surrender to raiders in some areas.

Elsewhere, resistance forced the raiders to desist in their activities. Bede notes (1.14):

> When the depredations of its enemies had ceased, the land enjoyed an abundance of corn without precedent in former years, but with plenty came an increase in luxury, followed by every kind of crime … Suddenly, a terrible plague struck this corrupt people, and in a short while destroyed so large a number that the living could not bury the dead … they consulted how they might obtain help to avoid or repel the frequent fierce attacks of their northern neighbours, and all agreed with the advice of their king, Vortigern, to call on the assistance of the Saxon peoples across the sea.

In Book 1, chapter 15, Bede recounts that in the period AD 449–456:

> The Angles or Saxons came to Britain … in three longships, and were granted lands in the eastern parts of the island on condition that they protected the country: nevertheless their real intention was to subdue it. They engaged the enemy advancing from the north, and having defeated them, sent back news of their success to their homeland.… Whereupon a larger fleet quickly came over with a great body of warriors, which, when joined to the original forces, constituted an invincible army. These also received from the Britons grants of land where they could settle among them on condition that they maintained the peace and security of the island against all enemies in return for regular pay.

Here, Bede seems to be describing phases of settlement, firstly of military *foederati* and subsequently infillings into the landscape of *laeti*. He describes them further:

> The newcomers were from the three most formidable races of Germany, the Saxons, Angles and Jutes. From the Jutes are descended the people of Kent and the Isle of Wight and those in the province of the west Saxons opposite the Isle of Wight who are called Jutes to this day. [It is clear from their similarities on these points that the *ASC* is based on Bede's narrative] … Their first chieftains are said to have been the brothers Hengist and Horsa. The latter was subsequently killed in a battle against the Britons, and was buried in east Kent, where a monument bearing his name still stands. … It was not long before such hordes of these alien peoples vied together to crowd into the island that the natives who had invited them began to live in terror.

Bede continues by describing an alliance between the Picts and the Angles, who then turned on their fellow Germanic settlers and 'these heathen conquerors devastated the surrounding cities and countryside, extended the conflagration from the eastern to the western shores'. Those native British not 'butchered wholesale' were 'doomed to lifelong slavery' or 'eked out a wretched and fearful existence among the mountains, forests and crags'. Perhaps it is optimistic to suggest that these conflagrations had moved beyond the bounds of Kent by this time, but it must be acknowledged that the general lack of archaeological evidence for Sub-Roman populations in this area cannot preclude their inclusion in this awful fate.

There is one piece of evidence that strikes a discordant note here and that is the naming of the territory of Kent. As Alec Detsitcas identifies, the name *Cantiaci* was a construct of the Romans, when forming a canton within the tribal area of the *Atrebates*. Yet, this name persists for both the area and the central place of Canterbury beyond the end of Roman control and is adapted, as *Cantware* into the name of the Anglo-Saxon kingdom, in contrast to the apparent wholesale take-over of both language and the naming of places by the Germanic incomers as evidenced elsewhere throughout Britain.

Can we accept at face value Bede's assertion of the Kentish settlers as emanating from Jutland and are we correct in locating this area in mainland Denmark? Bede was perhaps better informed about the history of Kent than for other regions, due to his ecclesiastical contacts in Canterbury. Nevertheless, doubts about the true content of his statement are an enduring problem in early Anglo-Saxon research, although J.N.L. Myres is astute in suggesting that perhaps Bede was referring to a more general cultural region in southern Scandinavia that included Jutes and Angles.

Still accepting the premise of mass movements across the North Sea, one must ask how people travelled and by what routes. The shortest crossing to Dover was clearly an important point of entry, but archaeology provides evidence of fifth-century material around the coast either side of there, with the inlets and estuaries from the Thanet, Sheppey and the Medway to the River Thames particularly well used. The types of seagoing craft that might have been used can be inferred from not-quite contemporary examples of archaeologically recovered boats. The three vessels from Nydam Moss on the island of Als in southern Denmark have been dated though tree-ring analysis (dendrochronology) to the mid-fourth century. Essentially these were long keeled rowing boats, of clinker built construction, in which overlapping strakes were fixed with iron rivets and roves. They were probably propelled by crews of 20–30 oarsmen, with little evidence for the use of sail. There are variations in their structures and types of timber used (oak and pine) pointing to diverse shipbuilding traditions in northern Europe. The relatively shallow drafts of these vessels indicate that they would have been beached on the shore with the tide, rather than requiring fixed wharfs and deep water. Their capacity for crossing open water is in dispute, more likely to have been used for coastal, short distance work, although given good sea and weather conditions this type of craft must have been used for the transportation of numbers of people and their chattels across the Channel.

Recent research into the genetic evidence for a Germanic migration during the fifth and sixth centuries has focussed on both maternal mitochondrial DNA and male Y-chromosomes as a way of tracking population movements in the past. Research into the latter has suggested that the best-fit model to explain the Y-chromosome variation in the modern English gene pool would be to consider the presence of a significant 'immigrant' (around twenty per cent) population during the Early Anglo-Saxon period, at least in eastern England which bears strong statistical similarities in genetic markers with Friesland. Potentially supporting this idea, population estimates based on burial evidence from Kent suggest an exponential growth of around 0.26 per cent per annum over the course of the period AD 475–750, which is roughly equivalent to that suggested for early modern societies. However, most of the excavated burials in Kent probably date to *c.*AD 500–700 and it is to this more contracted period that the population increase most likely dates, with the effects of 'incoming' populations on gross numbers more pronounced. More conservative estimates for the scale of the Anglo-Saxon settlement have been suggested by Stephen Oppenheimer in *The Origins of the British: A Genetic Detective Story* (London, 2006), who argues there are clear indications of a continuing indigenous component in the English paternal makeup, but nevertheless suggests that up to a fifteen per cent increase in genetic markers in parts of eastern Britain are attributable to a Germanic migration of the early medieval period. If, as some geneticists argue, this increase must be modelled within a time frame of only one or two generations, it certainly represents a significant genetic input. By way of comparison, modern mass-migrations such as that following the Rwandan crisis of 1994, altered the overall population of neighbouring Zaire by only 3.06 per cent, and Tanzania by 2.03 per cent, albeit over a very short time frame. Perhaps further complicating the issue, another genetic study by Foster *et al.* applied to language suggests that English diverged from Germanic languages before the fifth century; the implication being that eastern England at least already had long-standing contacts with the German-speaking world. Whatever the precise mechanism of migration one cannot avoid the assertion that, for

Germanic genetic material to have such a marked presence, a degree of social engineering must have taken place to actively inhibit the reproductive capacities of the indigenous male population.

The settlement

The documentary sources give us little further detail regarding the settlement of migrants in Kent. What, then, can the archaeological evidence tell us? Although, as we shall see, Kent of the sixth and seventh centuries is one of the richest sources in the whole of British archaeology, frustratingly the fifth century is only fleetingly present within the corpus. Essentially we can draw on three sources: the locations in the landscape of the earliest dated sites and objects, the form and content of the burials and the provenance of the grave goods.

A popular misconception about the fifth-century migrations into Kent has been to characterise the incomers in terms of heroic settlers colonising a barren and deserted landscape (*Fig. 9*). Key to this view, as a parallel to that of European settlers in the New World of Virginia, was the image of a woodland environment that had to be cleared and a new order imposed. The amount of place-names in Kent that have woodland elements in them (such as those ending in -den, from the Old English *denn*, -ley from *lēah*, -hurst from *hyrst*, and so on) would appear to support this view. Whilst woodland regeneration within previously arable areas is an inevitable consequence of abandonment of that form of agriculture, these conditions are not held to be accurate throughout the whole area of the Anglo-Saxon settlement. As Oliver Rackham has pointed out, those areas that were wooded enclaves in the Roman and earlier periods probably remained so for the Anglo-Saxons, for example the wood known as Cudham Frith, nestling in the North Downs between Bromley and Westerham, was probably delineated as far back as the Iron Age, if not earlier still. Only in the central Kentish tract of the Weald were there still areas of wildwood, or untouched natural forest, although parts of it had probably been managed as coppice to support the Roman ironworking industries and for transhumance, the seasonal pasturing of livestock on acorns and beech mast. Blean wood, still the largest single ancient woodland in Kent, was previously a much larger forest dominating the area between Faversham and Canterbury.

The incomers settled on the prime agricultural land that had been in use under the Romans, rather than on any marginal soil types, in the coastal *pays* and in the valley of the Holmesdale, termed the 'Original Lands' (*Fig. 10*). It is

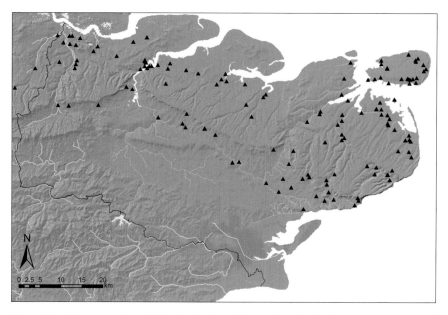

Fig. 10. Kentish topography and the distribution of the earliest Anglo-Saxon cemetery sites of the fifth and sixth centuries

not possible to identify much about their subsistence practices other than to suggest that they probably carried out a mixed farming regime, combining arable and animal husbandry, although the coastal and riverine locations of the earliest evidence from archaeology suggests that they engaged in trading and fishing activities too. Settlement evidence is sparse in comparison to that of the furnished burials. An early site was found in 1970 at Lower Warbank, Keston, adjacent to a Roman trackway through the North Downs and on a substantial Roman villa, during a training dig by the West Kent Group. It can only be dated to the period AD 450–550 and comprises a single example of a type of hut peculiar to the Anglo-Saxons, termed a sunken-featured build-ing or *Grubenhaus*, most likely used as a weaving shed. The remainder of the potential settlement area was left unexcavated. The animal bones from the site suggest a pastoral farming regime, whilst the pottery resembles material found at Saxon sites such as Mucking on the Thames Estuary, rather than anything distinctively Kentish as found across the Medway.

The dating of any of the archaeological material is fraught with problems, hence the broad date range for this and many other sites (*Fig. 11*). Essentially, for the determination of absolute and relative dates Kentish archaeology has been dependent on the use of Continental chronologies, wherein their association to coins can date objects. Given that coinage was not in use in

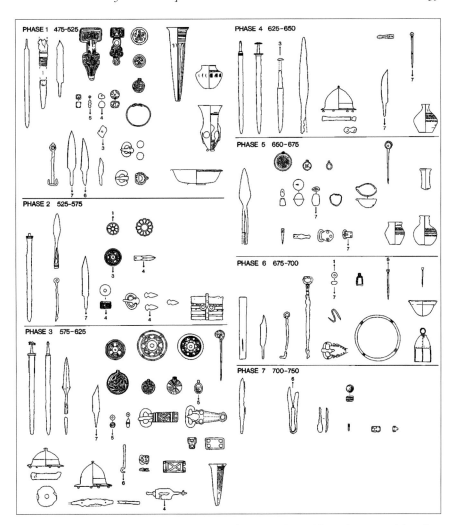

Fig. 11. Vera Evison's phases of Anglo-Saxon artefact types, derived from the material found at her excavation at Buckland, Dover in 1953. Reproduced from the excavation report, with permission

Kent until the seventh century this is not possible here. In addition it remains likely that there was a time lag of perhaps one or two generations between the use of objects on the Continent and their migration and deposition in Kent. Currently our dating schema in Kent begins around AD 450, although ongoing work and more finds may push back our assumptions in this regard. This start date does introduce a gap between the end of the Roman period and the beginning of the Germanic settlement.

The settlement of lowland Britain as a whole is best evidenced by the different burial practices of what we assume to have been the distinct tribal groupings. Within the eastern area that became East Anglia, cremation was predominant, reflecting the practices in the north German homelands, although the use of inhumation developed throughout the period. In the Thames Valley, a major point of entry to Britain, the settlers inhumed their dead in the Roman manner, suggesting an established relationship with the late Roman Empire, although cremation is also much in evidence in the early part of the period. In Kent east of the Medway, cremation is scantily evidenced in the fifth century, whereas inhumation with grave goods was the predominant burial rite, as it was in Jutland. It is to there that we must look for evidence, in terms of burial practices and the types of weapons, dress fitments and tools associated with them, to see if these are replicated in Kentish cemeteries.

The excavated and published cemetery at Sejlflod, on the east coast of the Jutland peninsula, provides such a resource, with over 300 furnished graves (although little in the way of skeletal remains) dating to the fourth and fifth centuries, that is, broadly contemporary with the supposed migration to Kent. Looking at this and other resources, researchers have carried out comparative studies. Birte Brugmann notes in her discussions of the earliest Kentish cemeteries, however, that 'not a single well-furnished inhumation … could confidently be labelled as that of an immigrant Jute', whilst the fragmentary archaeological evidence for the fifth century 'does not allow any reconstruction of a "first generation" of invaders, dressed and buried traditionally'. But it is not completely necessary to dismiss Bede's account in this context on the basis of the negative archaeological evidence. Frank Stenton points out that the Jutes and the Rhineland Franks may well have been connected and that the Jutes may have arrived in Kent from the mouth of the Rhine. It is reasonable to suggest that this geographical displacement would have had an impact on the material culture and perhaps on the burial traditions of the Jutes, although their self-identity as a coherent group and ideas about their ethnic origin would have remained intact.

Mixed rite cemeteries with a footprint in the fifth century, such as at Poverest Road Orpington, feature to the west of the Medway and again are more clearly related to the areas of Saxon settlement. A recent excavation at Ringlemere Farm, between Ash and Eastry, has for the first time produced an unambiguous mixed rite cemetery in East Kent and has been dated from about AD 450, going out of use about a hundred years later. It focuses on a prehistoric burial mound, a type of feature that recurs in use throughout the pagan Saxon period.

Those burials that can conclusively be placed in the fifth century fall into two rather small groups (as described by Andrew Richardson). For the first half of the century there are a few that have no distinctively Anglo-Saxon

Fig. 12. An example of Quoit Brooch Style. This buckle loop with fixed plate was found in a burial at the mixed rite cemetery at Poverest Road, Orpington and shows the distinctive range of motifs used in this style

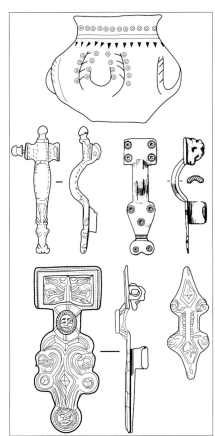

Fig. 13. Early Germanic style artefacts found in Kentish burials. From the top: a hand-made pot with stamped decoration (*Buckelurne*), cruciform brooch, small long brooch, Jutlandic bow brooch and equal arm brooch. Cruciform brooch reproduced from the excavation report, with permission

objects, rather containing Late Roman military belt sets and Quoit Brooch style metalwork (*Fig. 12*). The Quoit Brooch itself is a broad banded annular brooch with a distinctive 'notch and stops' fastening method, with a widespread distribution in Britain. The style to which it gives its name is rather more difficult to pin down and has been given to an extensive range of metalwork objects similarly widely spread, including buckles and belt sets, whose common feature is a range of insular punched and chip carved motifs that lie somewhere between Late Roman provincial decorative techniques and the emerging Germanic zoomorphic Style I.

Stronger evidence appears in the second half of the century, where early Germanic objects make a more definite appearance in the form of equal-armed brooches, Scandinavian relief brooches, early types of the cruciform, small long brooches and hand-thrown pottery vessels (*Fig. 13*). Examples of these have been excavated from Orpington, Buckland Dover and at Bifrons. Caution must be introduced here in that some at least of these early objects may have been curated and deposited in burials a generation or two after their manufacture, and may not genuinely reflect fifth-century burials.

Perhaps here is a good place to finally mention another group of people who may have impacted on the Anglo-Saxon settlement, the Frisians. Their position along the seaboard between the mouths of the Weser and the Rhine probably came under pressure from those migrating from further north seeking to gain access to the short sea route across to Kent. Bede makes reference to them in another section of his text as being one of the settling groups in Britain, but whilst there is plenty of Frisian type pottery found around the south-east coast of Britain, there is little other early evidence until they are seen to make an impact in the development of cross-Channel trade two centuries later.

Conclusion

How might we characterise the events of the fifth century in Kent? By the end of the century, a Germanic material culture was dominant, even though the settlements were often in proximity to Roman sites, with Roman landscape structures still in use. Whether a structured, hierarchical society had developed by then is questionable. It is more likely that kin and tribal allegiances were to the fore, as people settled in propinquity in optimum environmental locations. For the sub-Roman population, looking back on the century we can characterise their experience as one of crisis and dynamic transition into new ways of social being and culture. Regardless of the precise timescales of the events that took place, the final outcome of Germanic dominance was irrevocable and permanent. Whether we can identify a central authority in the fifth century actively assigning land grants to settlers, as opposed to an organic migration of land-hungry displaced tribes people, will remain open to question. The density of known settlements in the 'Original Lands' suggests that population pressure could have led to conflict, with the remnant sub-Roman households marginalized further. The extent to which the incomers used existing exchange systems, be they local or cross-Channel, or developed their own new versions can be seen more clearly in the sixth century. Regardless, the fundamental shift from sub-Roman to Anglo-Saxon Kent had been made.

CHAPTER 3

FROM MULTI-CULTURE TO KENTISH CULTURE: AD 500–580/90

Introduction

Documentary sources are for the most part silent on this important period of Kentish development, giving it a status as a 'Dark Age'. As mentioned in the previous chapter, this is a term used in the modern era to indicate an absence of historical sources, although previously used to highlight a barbarous Pagan period before the re-emergence of Christianity in Britain. But what was Kentish society really like before the Christian Mission arrived at King Æthelberht's court in AD 597?

Certainly, in 597 Kent appears a powerful and fully formed kingdom; that is to say under the control of a ruling elite. Through processes as yet undetermined, parts of the population must therefore at some stage have bound themselves together under the leadership of dominant kin groups. Accompanying this hardening of the social structure we see also the emergence of a distinctively Kentish material culture, evidence of a new kind of ostentatious identity. In Richard Hodges' view, the economic institutions of the Germanic tribes were primarily focused on central persons, in contrast to the Roman economy that was based on central places, and it is in the cult of personality that the emergence of a Kentish kingdom is perhaps to be sought.

This provides us with one way of exploring the dynamic and fast-moving changes that occured in the sixth century through to AD 590. Can we see in the sources, for example, the emergence of particular types of individuals or groups who expressed enhanced wealth or status, or other special means of identity? Can we provide a backdrop for the emergence of these people in the wider political, economic and social developments of the time?

In comparison with the remainder of lowland Britain, Kent was exceptionally wealthy, depositing more objects per head into the burial, with various forms and raw materials. It had access to a wide range of agrarian and marine resources, with some of the best soils and wide tracts of woodlands within its domain.

Unfortunately our two principal English sources for the period are both much later in date – the *Anglo-Saxon Chronicle*, first compiled in the late ninth century at the court of Alfred the Great, and the venerable Bede's *Historia Ecclesiastica*, completed in the early 730s – and therefore cannot be regarded as fully reliable accounts of Dark Age events. Some contemporary mid sixth-century observations of England are made from Gaul, but these provide only fragmentary and oblique insights into the political reality of the period. If anything, the one-sided nature of the early sources has often influenced our understanding of North Sea culture, colouring it from a distinctly Frankish world-view, which has significant implications for our understanding of Kentish society in the sixth century.

Given the state of written information, our sources for the period are primarily archaeological, from furnished burials and a small range of habitation sites, and include material found outside of the county of Kent, on mainland Europe and further north and west in Britain in the area of Anglo-Saxon settlement, indicating the reach of Kentish cultural, economic and political contacts. This evidence attests to the emergence of a distinctive Kentish culture with wide-reaching international links. At this time Kent was clearly closely bound to the Frankish kingdom across the Channel – its nearest neighbour – demonstrated by the evidence of a sprinkling of wealthy incomers wearing their characteristic belt fittings and brooches, whilst others had multi-cultural assemblages combining Frankish artefacts, together with Jutish and Scandinavian objects, prompting the naming of this period by researchers as the 'Frankish Phase' of influence. But the evidence, particularly from burial, can also be read to provide important insights into the character and form of Kentish society in the sixth century.

Archaeology is centrally placed to examine the social structure, emerging hierarchies and access to wealth of the Kentish communities as a whole and by key groups in particular. This chapter is structured to examine external influences on the Kentish kingdom, the situation within Kent itself, and the influence of Kent on the wider area of Germanic settlement in lowland Britain as a means of placing these changes within a wider context.

External influences

During the sixth century, the kingdom of Francia, under the control of the Merovingian dynasty, wielded enormous political, military and economic influence throughout northwestern Europe, conquering the Thuringians to the east across the Rhine in AD 531 and the Burgundians to the southeast in AD 532. Separated from the Frankish coast by only 34km, Kent is sure to have been affected by these circumstances, but it is unclear to what extent Francia overshadowed its near neighbour.

Frankish sources, perhaps reflecting their bias, suggest that Kent too may have been under the control of the Merovingians. Garbled testimony for Frankish authority in England has been interpreted from a reading of Procopius, who is assumed to have received reliable information regarding Frankish northern policy from the Frankish delegation to Constantinople in *c.*AD 553. He records a curious tale that shipments were regularly ferried from the port of Boulogne to an island of dead souls in *Brittia* (presumably Britain). Ian Wood believes that Procopius has confused the Greek word *thanatos* (dead) with the place-name 'Thanet', suggesting that the Franks demanded this transhipment as a service from the mariners living opposite the island, that is on mainland Kent. A further tale relates that the embassy of AD 553 also included Angles, who had been resettled within the Frankish kingdom,

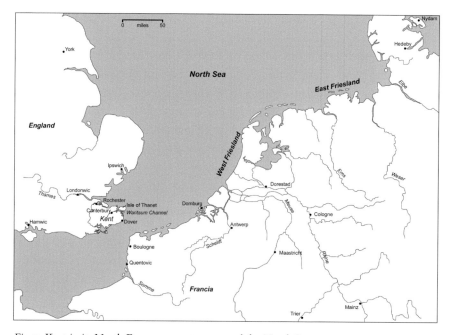

Fig. 14. Kent in its North European context around the North Sea

thus demonstrating Frankish overlordship of *Brittia*. Additional evidence for Merovingian claims over Kent can be interpreted from the *Pactus Legis Salicae* (39, 2) dating to the end of Clovis' reign, which legislates the procedures to be followed in foreign courts for the return of *servi* who had been carried off *trans mare*. Clovis was the first to unite the Frankish tribes through conquest under a single ruler, reigning from AD 485 to AD 511.

These records can be interpreted in a number of ways. The maximalist explanation might see all of the social and political developments in Kent during this period as a result of expansionist policies in contemporary Francia. Central to this argument is an assertion that Kent developed as a peripheral state to its more powerful neighbour, who through its military and economic might imposed itself over much of the southern North Sea region during this period. Proponents of this view argue that developments in Francia under the Merovingian dynasty drove many of the changes visible particularly in Kent and the Low Countries, and that the fortunes of these regions were intimately linked to those of Francia.

Taken together these sources may record Frankish political aspirations rather than reality, although plenty of archaeological evidence exists to propose significant cross-Channel connections throughout the sixth century between Kent and Francia. That these Frankish kings claimed sovereignty over Kent at least indicates the existence of a Frankish fleet with which they could enforce their authority if necessary – although Procopius' narrative suggests regular commercial activity between the two unequal polities. Clovis' legislation adds a third dimension. If *trans mare* can be assumed to mean Kent, the appearance of Frankish slaves in that kingdom could imply that relations between the two kingdoms may not have been entirely amicable. Alternatively, enslaved Franks may have been returned to their homeland via Kent, after abductions by other Anglo-Saxon raiders. A further, less violent explanation finds analogy in current political events: Clovis' legislation may simply relate to stowaway slaves on cross-Channel vessels – people returned to their point of origin, having previously fled to seek a safer or better life in Britain.

The Frankish Phase

Archaeological proponents of this term have argued that the links between Francia and Britain are visible in a pattern of exchanged goods and material culture that are at their most demonstrable in Kent. The relative absence of Frankish goods in other areas of lowland Britain indicates that Kent may have created a trade monopoly with elements of the earlier established Frankish kingdoms across the Channel. The contact was visibly instrumental

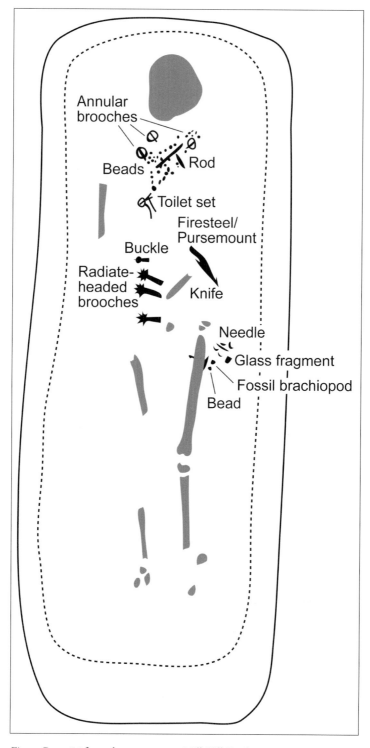

Fig. 15. Grave 86 from the cemetery at Mill Hill, Deal

in the maintenance of the Kentish kingdom, which Sonia Chadwick
Hawkes, somewhat controversially, sees as fully formed by the early part of
the sixth century, including the annexation of West Kent (see below). The
Kentish trading links encompassed, in the first half of the sixth century, the
Charente region (evidenced exclusively by Kentish objects from the extraor-
dinarily rich Frankish cemetery inland at Herpes, archived in the British
Museum), western Normandy, the Rhineland, Frisia, Thuringia and southern Scandinavia. Kentish material is consistently present in the Merovingian
cemeteries of the North Sea coastal regions of Francia, for example at Vron
and at Nouvion, both in Picardy. It has been suggested that these objects represent settlement in northern France by kin groups from southern England,
although given that the coastal area may also have been settled by federate
troops in the Late Roman period, these may be peoples with a common
Germanic ancestry. Perhaps we may begin to think of a North Sea littoral in
the sixth century, influenced by Saxons and Jutes rather than wholly dominated by Franks.

The relative absence of Kentish artefacts is notable in the area between the
Seine and the Somme, that is, directly across the Channel from a region of
Saxon settlement in Sussex, and is evidence that further underlines the presence of links in this period between discrete groups rather than exchange
routes open to all comers. Any trade monopoly may have been forcibly
controlled, perhaps explaining the prevalence of male weapon graves in
the coastal areas of Kent. Trade may have been facilitated through private
arrangements, which were cemented by patrilocal exogamous intermar-
riage, that is females moving from their own domicile to that of their new
husband's kin. Such a system of kin group alliances might explain the occurrence in Kent of Frankish grave goods and dress styles, such as gold braided
feminine headbands. Key artefact types that illustrate the Frankish presence
include radiate-headed brooches, bird brooches, shield-on-tongue buckles,
kidney shaped iron buckles with silver wire inlay and rosette garnet disc
brooches (*Plate 7*). An example of a possible Frankish marriage bride is the
woman in grave 86 at Mill Hill, Deal (*Fig. 15*), dressed for the burial with
three radiate-headed brooches, provenanced to the Frankish Middle Rhine.
It was more common, however, for the Frankish brooches to be used in
combinations of types. The abrupt disappearance of Frankish feminine jew-
ellery from grave assemblages after *c.*AD 560 has been linked to the accession
of Æthelbehrt to the Kentish throne and a suppression of private enterprise
through the imposition of a royal monopoly on trade, as argued by Sonia
Chadwick Hawkes.

Southern Scandinavia

Links with the southern Scandinavian homelands of the settlers in Kent were probably maintained by marriage, given that artefacts originating from these areas are found mainly in female graves. They belong in the sixth century to a secondary phase of settlement, dubbed the 'establishment phase', wherein the descendants of key families sought ideologically important ethnic symbols to legitimise and reinforce their, perhaps newly elevated, social position. These symbols could take the form of inherited heirlooms, locally produced pseudo-ethnic metalwork and constructed symbolic assemblages and rituals.

Three artefact types are important here, amongst others: bracteates, bow brooches and iron weaving swords. The most numerous group of objects are the gold bracteates (*Plate 8*), die stamped pendants that have been recovered throughout England and the Continent, with forty-two examples coming from Kent out of a total of fifty-two known from the region south of the Thames. Bracteates internationally number approximately 900 and are derived from 500 different die stamps. In Britain they generally conform to four of the seven known types: A – showing a human face, in a similar format to that of antique imperial coins; B – one to three human figures in various positions, often with animals; C – showing a man's head above a four-legged animal (the most common find and often interpreted as representing the god Woden); and D – showing several animals. They originate in southern Scandinavia, where they are found primarily in hoards, such as that from the farmstead at Gudme, Fyn, Denmark (on display in the National Museum in Copenhagen), but by c.AD 530/40 had ceased to be manufactured there. Usually found in the burial incorporated into bead necklaces, occasionally with pierced Roman coins, their significance was clearly non-monetary, but not necessarily non-economic. None have been found on settlement sites in Kent to date. They can be seen as a medium for both creating and maintaining social and political relations through personal gift giving and as such might be characterised as special-purpose tokens. For those able to understand the iconography, they would indicate the personal linkages between the many small kingdoms within that region and beyond. This particular use of coins and bracteates appears to be a translation of Roman customs and means of exchange, evidenced, for example, in the earlier Roman use of gifts to obtain valuable trade goods such as hides from the Baltic island of Öland. The distribution of bracteates in northern and central Europe mirrors those groups maintaining Scandinavian connections throughout their diaspora, for example the Langobards, who eventually settled in central Italy, and are interpreted as cohesive markers of political loyalty and identity in times of diverse cultural influences.

Fig. 16. The weaving sword from Sarre grave 4, showing the short-tipped end. The tang for the wood or bone handle is missing. Image courtesy of Maidstone Museum and Art Gallery

Within Kent and East Anglia, the two main distribution areas in England, bracteates appear in burial assemblages from the early sixth century. Very few are the products of the same dies, with multiple types appearing on the same necklace, indicating accumulation processes taking place. No C bracteates are known from Kent, with the only known B bracteate in Britain coming from Bifrons grave 29. Kent produced what some have viewed as domestic copies of Scandinavian D bracteates, with the production of new types continuing into the seventh century. As a group, there are links between the dies used for the bracteates found in Bifrons graves 29 and 64 and Lyminge grave 16, and an association probably existed between these and the four well-made items from Finglesham graves D3 and 203. Whether the bracteates found in England were from a batch production carried out at a single point of origin, either locally or in Scandinavia, and held as heirlooms over time with sequential deposition in the grave, or were the products of curated dies and manufactured sequentially over time, remains a matter for conjecture. In the context of this discussion, it is significant to note the coincidence in East Kent, but not elsewhere in early Anglo-Saxon England, of bracteates with iron weaving-swords.

Sword-shaped weaving beaters first originated in central and southern Norway in the third century AD (*Fig. 16*). Their resemblance to weapon swords is passing, in that they are much shorter and lighter, have blunt edges and a distinctive short tip at one end, although with a comfortable grip handle of bone or wood at the other. They were most probably used for beating up the weft on a warp-weighted loom, to produce lengths of densely woven cloth, possibly not used for clothing but for a more rugged purpose. Of twenty-one known examples from lowland Britain, thirteen are from burials in East Kent, where they developed over the space of two or three generations (a generation taken as approximately twenty-five years) into a distinctive Kentish type, slightly differently proportioned to contemporary objects in Norway, the Rhineland and Alamannia. It is perhaps important to note that this tool type has not been found in contemporary Jutlandic archaeological contexts. The earliest dated Kentish find, from the child in Buckland, Dover grave 20, most closely resembles the Norwegian types, but thereafter they become longer and are on occasion pattern-welded like weapon swords or are examples of re-used and re-worked swords. They disappear from the burial assemblages probably by c.AD 580.

The third major group of objects are Jutlandic bow brooches. In general form they are square-headed brooches with a flat decorated disc on the bow. Although the square headed style of brooch develops in lowland Britain, with Kent taking a lead, the earliest examples appear to have come from Jutland, although many show signs of long-term use before their inclusion in the burial assemblages here. Notable examples again come from Bifrons grave 64 and Finglesham grave 203. Detailed comparative analysis of the craftsmanship that produced a range of brooches has led to the proposal that a single 'Kentish Master' may have been responsible, working first in Jutland at the end of the fifth century, then later relocating to Kent, perhaps with

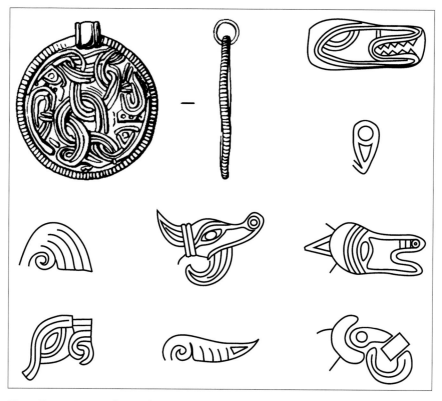

Fig. 17. Recurring motifs in Style I, comprising elements of the head, body and feet of animals, some of which are displayed on the bracteate from grave 1, Buckland, Dover, reproduced from the excavation report, with permission

one or two others, to develop a wider array of finely crafted dress fitments in silver, copper alloy, gold and garnet. Here perhaps we should address the issue of Style I, which is very much a central element of this phase of Kentish cultural development.

Style I (*Fig. 17*), as determined by Bernhard Salin in 1904, is the initial phase of three describing the development of Germanic zoomorphic ornamentation. Style I has a broad repertoire of design elements, with an emphasis on the discrete parts of animal bodies, within a naturalistic format. It does not stand alone, however, but appears as a development of Late Roman chip-carving style, via the Nydam style (with its stronger Nordic feel), which combined different types of animal, depicting, for example, a sea monster as a quadruped and with the head of a raptor. Other strong and distinctive elements in Style I are the introduction of contour lines to each body part and the rounded relief of the animals. Why the change from a style characterised by sea monster motifs to one composed of diffuse body parts of quadrupeds should have taken place and what meanings can be attached to this must remain an ongoing discussion. At the heart must have been a set of mythological and religious beliefs that found no room for expression as the century drew to a close – and here we see the transposition into Style II. Nevertheless, Style I developed in the Scandinavian homelands and flourished in Kent, perhaps using the brooches from Jutland as templates to be embellished.

Other European contacts

Although the majority of non-Kentish objects came from Francia and to a lesser extent southern Scandinavia, either as curated or new objects, there are hints at wider links too. Glass vessels such as claw beakers in particular were probably imported from the lower Rhineland, and it is likely that the necklace sets of monochrome and polychrome glass beads were not locally produced either. To this catalogue we might add faceted rock crystal spindle whorls, which had a very broad European wide distribution and were probably traded through Francia from a source further to the east. Amber beads, found singly or in festoons of up to 160, probably came, perhaps indirectly, from the Baltic. Textiles, although fleetingly surviving into the archaeological record, similarly demonstrate a range of local and international sources. A rosette twill from Finglesham grave 203, used to cover a copper-alloy bowl, was probably an import from the Alamannic region of southwest Germany. A bow brooch in Bifrons grave 76 came from Thuringia, amongst a few examples.

Kent: AD 500–575

The Kentish economy and means of exchange

The prosperity of Kent in the first three quarters of the sixth century must have been based on an exchange system entailing considerable wealth-generating capacity. A putative list of Kentish staple trade goods would suggest cloth, hides, furs, slaves and hunting dogs, with either a single good dominant or possibly a combination of these goods. We might also suggest cereals as an important staple trade good, but this is well nigh impossible to demonstrate archaeologically and there are no documentary references to support such an inference. By implication to its relationship with Francia, Kent could supply goods of an esoteric or quantitative nature that were unavailable to its trading partners. Furs and hunting dogs may perhaps be discounted as the economic basis underpinning this early state. Species prized for their fur, such as bear and beaver, were generally extinct in Britain by the historic period, although they survived in numbers in mainland Europe. The wolf may also have been in decline, perhaps surviving in the Weald, its presence incompatible with progressive settlement of the landscape, although retaining a mythic and metaphoric status in Anglo-Saxon literature. Hunting dogs, if important to Kent, might be expected to be noted in later literary sources, or to occur in graves at least in the same manner as the few horse burials, but none have been identified archaeologically. As burial with grave goods is taken as an indicator of status and socially important tasks, for example being a spearman, then huntsmen might also be acknowledged. The incidence of hunting equipment, such as angons (barbed - headed throwing spears) and arrows, is notably rare in this period and in any case is more usually associated with Frankish burial. The developing pattern of land use and settlement was essentially agrarian with transhumant elements and might be considered largely incompatible with the trapping and large-scale hunting of wild animals. The resources of the Weald, acting as a hinterland for the coastal settlements, would have included grazing, timber and iron. A Wealden iron industry may have been active on a small scale by the sixth century, although no direct continuity with the important Roman iron industry has been demonstrated archaeologically. Any analysis of Kentish burial goods in comparison with the rest of lowland Britain amply demonstrates that Kent was particularly wealthy in terms of iron, or at least that the people were prepared to consign significant quantities of this material into their grave assemblages.

The potential importance of the remaining elements on the list is more consistent with the historical and archaeological evidence. Any trade in slaves to mainland Europe would more easily be accomplished via the short

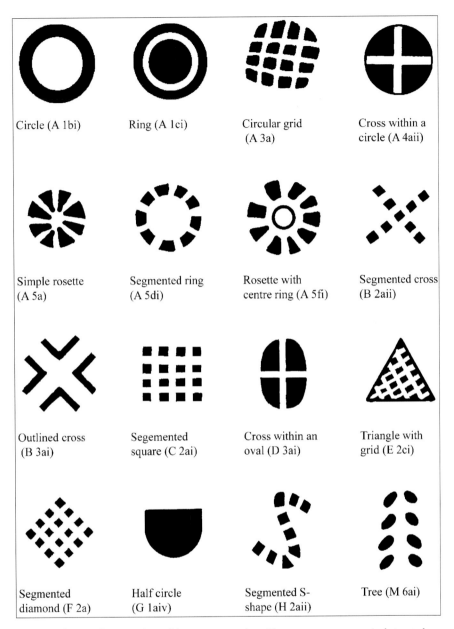

Circle (A 1bi)

Ring (A 1ci)

Circular grid (A 3a)

Cross within a circle (A 4aii)

Simple rosette (A 5a)

Segmented ring (A 5di)

Rosette with centre ring (A 5fi)

Segmented cross (B 2aii)

Outlined cross (B 3ai)

Segemented square (C 2ai)

Cross within an oval (D 3ai)

Triangle with grid (E 2ci)

Segmented diamond (F 2a)

Half circle (G 1aiv)

Segmented S-shape (H 2aii)

Tree (M 6ai)

Fig. 18. Only a small proportion of the pottery produced between AD 400–750 is decorated with stamps (i.e. a design impressed into the surface of the pot). There are fifteen sites in Kent where stamped pottery has been found, and these have produced fifty-nine motifs from eighty-five pots. Canterbury (with eighteen stamps), Northfleet (fifteen), and the Riseley Estate, Horton Kirby (fourteen) have produced over half the total. All the stamp motifs shown above have been found in Kent. Image courtesy of Diana Briscoe

sea route from Kent. The redistributive pattern of imported pottery vessels within Kent suggests a system of reciprocal tokens, with the pots or their contents being used in exchange for goods or people which the Kentish hierarchy could trade on to mainland Europe. The demand for labour to increase localised production of goods, particularly within Merovingian Neustria, across the Channel from Kent, in the sixth century, may have underpinned a trade in slaves and fuelled economic growth in the region. The demographic impact of a culling of the local population for export as slaves might well explain the perceived invisibility of the indigenous Romano-British people in the Kentish cemetery evidence.

The evidence for textiles and leather is also tentative, given their relative non-survival in archaeological contexts when compared to the range of metalwork and jewelled artefacts of the period. The landscape and settlement evidence for the early Anglo-Saxon period appears to suggest a significant role for sheep in the agrarian economy of the seventh century on the downlands, perhaps in an attempt to maximise productive capacity. Sunken-featured buildings (SFBs) dated to the sixth century regularly provide evidence of weaving processes having taken place there, although it is difficult to assess whether this was for domestic use or for limited surplus production to pay tribute to a local leader.

Studies of stamped and incise-decorated hand-made pottery vessels (*Fig. 18*) suggest that distributions of specific types, or stamp-groups, were geographically limited and therefore best explained by local production and distribution mechanisms, including transference by exogamy and local exchange. Exotic metalwork, on the other hand, is argued to reflect both specialist production and restricted social use. As such, their distribution is often implicitly understood within luxury-good exchange mechanisms, or as migratory heirlooms.

Kentish decorated metalwork

The emergent elites of the Kentish kingdom began to display specifically Kentish-made high status objects, conceivably in order to demonstrate their independence from Francia. Large-scale importation of silver into Kent in the second half of the sixth century is evidenced by the presence of silver square-headed and jewelled disc brooches. By far the greatest number of these brooches was found at King's Field, Faversham, when in the mid-nineteenth century the cutting for the railway line destroyed what had been perhaps the single richest cemetery site in Kent. Given the pivotal location of the site, at the junction of the London to Canterbury Roman road and at the head of a navigable creek with access to the Swale and the coastal route

(*Plate 9*), it is surmised that Faversham (a place name interpreted as deriving from the Latin *faber*, perhaps in reference to metal-working) was the place of manufacture of these items.

Within Kentish feminine graves there is a discernible stylistic change that marks a notional juncture between the Frankish phase and the Kentish phase. The new Kentish fashion (*Fig. 19*) utilised only one keystone-garnet disc brooch at the neck, whereas the continental fashion was for multiple brooches. This unique brooch type was an elaboration of the decorated discs on Jutlandic bow brooches and incorporated imported garnets, silver and gold foil. Whilst the decorated metal artefacts are abundant in the burials, the dating of them relies quite heavily on continental chronologies. The period of overlap between the first keystone-garnet disc brooches and final production of the Kentish square-headed brooches, can be dated as contemporary with the Frankish *Stufe* (phase) IIIa, AD 525–560.

There are a handful of famous sixth-century female burials from Kent, but these are at the extreme end of wealth and cluster temporally around the middle decades of the century. Sarre grave 4 is a case in point. This richly endowed, larger than average burial was probably that of an adult female, who died in the period AD 540–550. Her personal effects consisted of a necklace of six gold bracteates, all D type, with three possibly from the same die, two keystone-garnet disc brooches on either side of her chest and two small square-headed brooches further down. A crystal ball and a perforated spoon, set with garnets, were found at her knees, probably suspended from her waist. Over her body were found a scatter of beads, including 133 amber and others of glass. A length of gold braid ran from over her head and down her right arm, probably the edging to a veil or headdress. A spiral knot silver finger ring was located on her right hand. A pair of shears in a case, a knife with a decorated blade and two hook-shaped keys formed a chatelaine complex at her left waist. Other items, the position of which was not recorded by the excavator, included a Kentish/Frankish type copper-alloy shield-on-tongue buckle loop and two shoe shaped rivets, a copper-alloy tube (probably the handle of a small brush), a bone comb, a pin, a Roman coin, a fossil amulet and a bracelet. In addition she had had placed around her body an iron weaving-sword, alongside her left arm, a box with silver corner plates, position unknown and a glass bell beaker to the left of her head.

Hers was by far the most complex assemblage of the eighteen feminine burials dated to the sixth century from this site. It contained iron artefacts of local provenance, dress fitments originating in Francia and from the emerging Kentish metalwork culture together with bracteates from southern

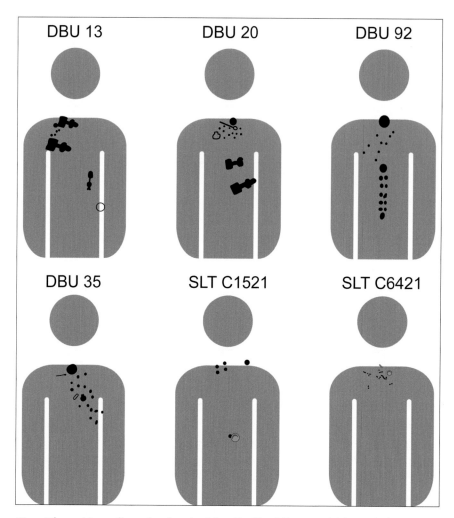

Fig. 19. The positions of brooches from burials at Buckland, Dover and Saltwood. The top row are from sixth-century finds, the bottom row from late sixth- to early seventh-century burials. The changing positions indicate changing styles in costume, although these are difficult to reconstruct in detail

Scandinavia. Thus, she embodied the full range of cultural elements available in East Kent in this period. Of her possible contemporaries in the Sarre cemetery, whilst each possessed significant Kentish and Frankish material, none had wealth sourced from southern Scandinavia, apart from the presence of amber beads. Sarre grave 4 had, however, 133 of these, the most in any one grave. The presence of additional objects around the body was uncommon amongst these women, thus underlining the effort and wealth associated with her interment.

Birte Brugmann, in her analysis of East Kent brooch type combinations, noted that D bracteates are only found with Jutish-Kentish and Kentish-Continental type brooches in rich feminine graves, whilst those other women wearing indigenous Anglo-Saxon brooch combinations did not stand out as particularly wealthy within the cemetery groups. Indeed other brooch types are consistently present, suggesting that women from other parts of lowland Britain lived and died in Kent. For example, the women in Lyminge grave 39 had a pair of saucer brooches, distinctive of the Saxon settlements of the Upper Thames Valley, which she combined with a pair of Kentish small square-headed brooches. Likewise the woman from Bifrons grave 77 had a pair of small long brooches, an Anglian/Saxon type, yet also wore a Kentish/Frankish type of copper-alloy buckle loop. Costume reconstruction in this phase is problematic, more so than, for example, with contemporary Saxon women whose brooch at each shoulder probably held up a peplos-style shift dress. Mixtures of local and foreign fashions may have been used to give a distinctive regional style, as evidenced by the wearing of brooch types from a range of Germanic sources, rather than as a clear ethnically determined kit.

Weapon burials

The focus on rich female dress fitments should not detract from the importance of male weapon burials in sixth-century Kent. Approximately seventy per cent of all burials dated to this phase, whether male or female, young or old, were furnished to a greater or lesser degree. Approximately half of all men were furnished with weapons, usually just a spear, but other combinations might include a sword and/or a shield. The geographical distribution of sword burials, those of the perceived highest status, merits comment. Over thirty sword burials can be confidently dated to the sixth century, with multiple sword burials in certain sites, for example four from Mill Hill, Deal, four from Sarre and three from Buckland, Dover. The coastal location of these cemeteries does indicate a powerful control of the maritime part of Kent by these communities (*Fig. 20*).

Located on a tidal inlet above the easterly entrance to the Wantsum Channel and not strictly speaking on the coast, the community at Finglesham usefully illustrates several salient points about the role of male weapon burials. The settlement, although not actually located by excavation, was probably at the head of a small creek leading off a larger, sheltered inlet that gave access by sea to the other settlements of the Wantsum Channel and the River Stour. The place name Finglesham has been interpreted to mean 'prince's manor or homestead', although the naming is not necessarily contemporary with the features discussed here. The community was probably founded in the first

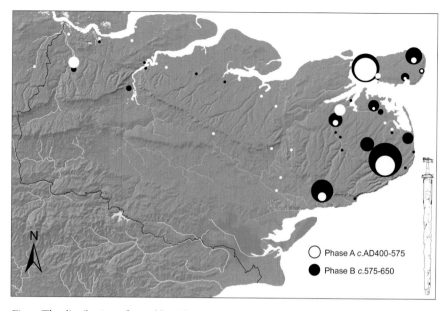

Fig. 20. The distribution of sword burials in Kent, comparing the fifth to sixth centuries with the late sixth and early seventh centuries. Note the heaviest concentrations over time are in the coastal regions nearest to mainland Europe. The sword from grave c, Buckland, Dover is reproduced from the excavation report, with permission

third of the sixth century, with the earliest female graves exhibiting southern Scandinavian links, although firmly Kentish a generation later. If the woman in grave D3 was one of the founders, her contemporary male in grave 204 must also be considered as such. Both were sited within a spaced group on the highest part of the site, overlooking the supposed settlement.

Grave 204 probably had a substantial barrow, enhancing its prominent position. The remains of a male aged about twenty-five were found within it. His weapons consisted of a Kentish type ring pommel sword and scabbard, a spearhead with ferrule and a shield, placed between his coffin (evidenced by nails and clamps) and the wall of the grave. His personal effects consisted of the ubiquitous knife, a leather bag or pouch and a distinctive early Frankish iron kidney-shaped buckle loop, set with garnets, glass and silver wire. This object shows considerable wear, whereas the sword was in pristine condition. In addition, he was furnished with a glass claw beaker and an embossed rim copper-alloy bowl. Clearly the founders were of an upper echelon, although the conjunction of Scandinavian, Frankish and Kentish elements might have many interpretations. Possession of a sword, however (and it is noted that weaving-swords such as D3's only occur if weapon swords are present and contemporary), suggests the granting of rights to land and potential control of routeways to an elite group. That there was an ongoing process of land allocation in the sixth century perhaps speaks of a controlling hand and hierarchy of access.

Gender relationships

It has been suggested by Sonia Chadwick Hawkes that the contemporary occupants of Finglesham D3 and 204 may have had a formalised relationship as founders of a dynastic group. Certainly there are sufficient elements to suggest a unification of two parties, with their mixture of Kentish, Frankish and southern Scandinavian markers. The issue of the social relations between genders in early Anglo-Saxon society, in terms of their formalised rights and responsibilities, has generally only been addressed through documentary sources that occur outside of the time frame of this proto-historic period. The *Germania* of Tacitus, written in the late first century AD and purporting to be an ethnography of Germanic peoples is necessarily a source of questionable relevance to the early Anglo-Saxons, yet echoes of its comments regarding marriage dowries recur in much later texts. Tacitus describes, in chapter 18, the dowry brought by the husband to the wife at marriage as consisting of 'oxen, a horse with its bridle, or a shield, spear and sword', which she must hand on intact to her children so that her son's wife shall receive them. The feminine role in the transmission of arms and wealth is visible still within the cognatic kinship in Anglo-Saxon England in the period of the seventh to eleventh centuries AD. Here we might find the means and the context through which Finglesham D3 and 204 were given their grave goods.

Multiple burials were relatively infrequent events, occurring either as contemporary parallel bodies or temporally different, stacked inhumations. It appears that parallel, multiple inhumations were the result of the simultaneous demise of people in an unknown relationship, but most frequently of the same sex. Indeed in most cases it can be surmised that they were generally unequal people, differing in age and status, a situation pertaining for both men and women. One of the few examples of mixed sex parallel burials in the same grave cut of the sixth century comes from Mill Hill Deal grave 105, dated AD 530–570. A thirty-five to forty-five-year-old male was laid alongside a thirty to forty-year-old female, with a juvenile (twelve to fourteen) of unknown sex between them. The female was clearly of high status, with gold braid and a mix of Kentish brooches and, unusually, the spear was located by her left shoulder rather than in direct association with the man. This arrangement should not be taken to indicate that she had warrior status. Rather, it is the presence of an element placed between the man and the woman, that is, the body of a juvenile that might have been a causal factor in the displacement of the spear. It may have been the case that the juvenile was the offspring of the man and woman. The woman may have been the means through which a spear might come into the man's possession, perhaps as a wedding gift and it may have reverted to her at death, to be passed on to the offspring's spouse in the afterlife.

One of the most unusual multiple inhumations nationally is that from grave 21 at Stowting. The parish of Stowting (*Plate 10*) is somewhat isolated in comparison to those others providing us with furnished inhumation cemeteries. Although looking out towards the coast and the Weald, it lies slightly away from the main routeways. The cemetery lay on the lower slopes of Stowting Hill, 100–150m OD and dates from the early sixth to the early seventh centuries, with approximately sixty-six graves uncovered to date. John Brent excavated grave 21, amongst others, in 1866. Here is an abridged version of his report:

> This was a remarkable grave, or rather vault. It contained six skeletons all lying nearly north and south. It was a circular shape, nearly 9' in diameter … The skeletons lay all at the same level. The skull of the second touched the left shoulder of the first … the skulls of the other four were parallel with the shoulder of the second internment … (they) lay so close together that there was great difficulty in distinguishing the special relics of each.

The special relics included keys, two spindle whorls, six copper alloy, silver and garnet brooches, finger rings, knives, buckles, tweezers, Roman coins (used in necklaces) and a large number of beads. It would appear that this was a group of women, with perhaps one or two of a higher status – wearing multiple brooches, rather than equally shared, although not as wealthy as those women found in cemeteries closer to the coast. We can only conjecture the circumstances of their demise in the first half of the sixth century, and an epidemic cannot be ruled out.

Curated Roman-ness

One of the spindle whorls in grave 21 at Stowting was a curated Roman object made of shale. It was a not uncommon practice to deposit Roman artefacts into the burial, perhaps, but not necessarily, a reflection of the continued use of these objects in life (*Fig. 21*). Most numerous were copper-alloy and occasionally silver Roman coins depicting the head of an emperor, pierced for suspension in a necklace. Other types include jet beads, glass bracelets, brooches, glass vessels (most numerous at Faversham), pottery vessels and keys. The smaller objects tended to be included in bag

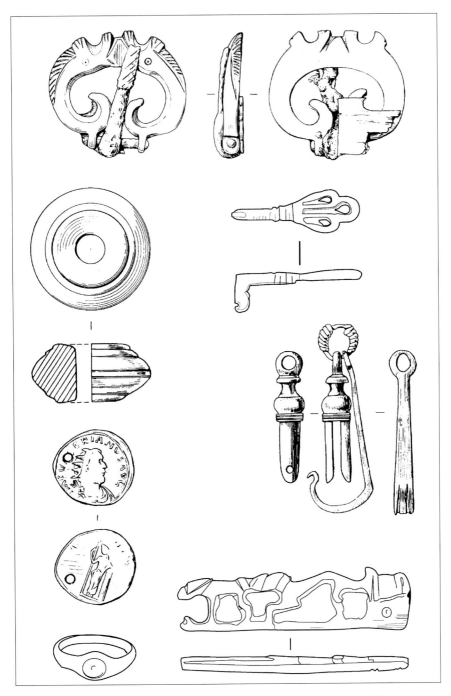

Fig. 21. Some Roman period items found in Anglo-Saxon burials at Buckland, Dover. From the top: a copper-alloy buckle loop with confronted dolphins, a shale spindle whorl, a key, a coin, a chatelaine suspension device, a finger ring and a knife handle. Finds reproduced from the excavation report, with permission.

or box collections, perhaps for their amuletic value, rather than used for their original purposes.

Settlements

Most of what we can identify about habitation in the sixth century has come from excavations within the major Roman and Medieval settlements of Canterbury and Dover. In Canterbury 'Dark Earth' deposits, uncovered in various locations within the city (such as the bus station and 3 Beer Cart Lane), suggest that a significant re-organisation of the Roman settlement took place during the fifth and sixth centuries. 'Dark Earth' is typically related to the abandonment of urban living and an increase in middening and agricultural activities, which suggest that the settlement that existed within Canterbury had become much more rural in character. In support of this conclusion, SFBs are known from the mid fifth century, and their location, in some places within ruined Roman masonry buildings, suggest at least a partial abandonment of the Roman streetscape at this time.

Apart from the evidence from Canterbury, some new minor sites of a rural character have emerged as a direct result of infrastructure building for the Channel Tunnel Rail Link, but this is still insufficient to give us a clear picture, leaving our interpretations dependent on other sources such as place-names and ecclesiastical history. In common with other major Roman centres nationally, we can point to a process of suburban reoccupation in the sixth century at Canterbury and possibly Dover. Nevertheless, any mapping of known sixth-century settlements reinforces the view propounded by Alan Everitt that the early zones of colonisation and settlement were the Foothill northern coastal strip and the fertile tracts of the Homesdale *pays*, linked by three river valleys – those of the Darenth, the Medway and the Stour, and termed by him as the Original Lands. Movement away from the earliest zone of settlement appears to have begun in the later sixth century.

The Kentish influence on lowland Britain, the Isle of Wight and the annexation of West Kent

Whilst Kent's primary relationship appears to have been with Francia, this did not preclude its own expansionist tendencies towards the rest of lowland Britain. Whilst it is difficult to characterise the nature of such tendencies in the sixth century, either as targeted activity led by a militaristic hierarchy already answerable to an overlord or as the activities of entrepreneurial kin groups working semi-autonomously, the archaeological evidence shows

Plate 1. Coastal erosion in action. Photograph demonstrating the precarious position of the Anglo-Saxon minster of Reculver and the remains of the Roman Saxon shore fort of *Regulbium* in which it is sited. Further emphasising the scale of erosion, a charter of the mid-tenth century makes clear that to the north (left) of the church there existed at that time an island – of which Black Rock is all that remains – separated from Reculver by the Bishopstone Brook

Plate 2. Members of the Bexley Archaeology Group at work digging and sorting finds on a local excavation. Visit http://www.bag.org.uk/ for more information

Plate 3. Charter documenting Godwine, Earl of Kent's grant of land to Leofwine the Red of certain swine-pastures at Swithrædingdænne (? Southernden, Kent), which Leofwine attaches to Boughton (? Malherbe), dated to 1013/1020. Reproduced from *Archaeologia Cantiana* 1

Plate 4. The remains of the Saxon shore fort of *Rutupiae* (Richborough). Image courtesy of Val Vannet, Creative Commons

Opposite from top

Plate 5. The collapsed Roman bridge in the River Medway at Rochester, recorded on underwater radar equipment used by the captain of the X-Pilot charter boat

Plate 6. The London to Lewes Roman road at Cudham, surviving as an earthwork. Here it forms part of the Kent/Surrey county boundary

Line of Roman Road

Plate 7. Frankish brooches found in Kentish female burials. Top row: radiate head brooches; bottom row: S-shaped brooch of two opposed backward biting animals, garnet disc and rosette brooch, bird brooch. Images courtesy of Maidstone Museum and Art Gallery

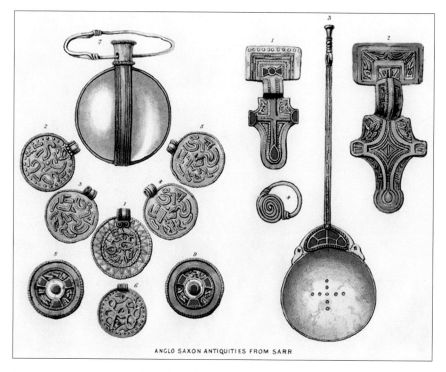

ANGLO SAXON ANTIQUITIES FROM SARR

Plate 8. Bracteates, crystal ball, perforated spoon and other personal effects from grave 4 at Sarre, dated to the mid-sixth century

Plate 9. The sand bar at the entrance to Faversham Creek, taken from mid channel in the Swale

Plate 10. A view across the site of the cemetery at Stowting, looking southeast towards the church and Cobb's Hill

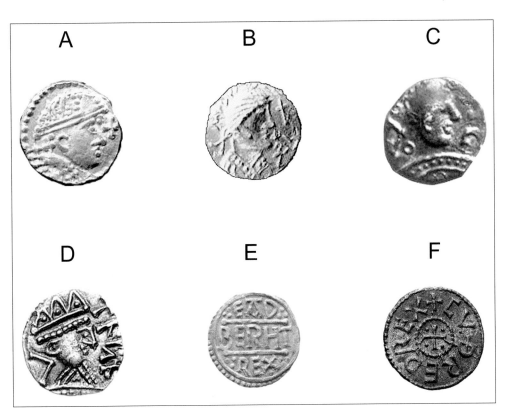

Plate 13. Kentish coins (obverse only): a) The earliest gold shillings clearly imitated Roman coinage, such as this Type Sutherland II.i from near Maidstone, dating to around 650–70 (EMC no. 2008.0030); b) Gold shillings of Æthelberht's son Eadbald are the earliest surviving coins in the name of an Anglo-Saxon king – he may have been responsible for promoting a new phase of coinage (EMC no. 1999.0004); c/d) Silver pennies or *sceattas*: c) a Series A from Horton Kirby, dating to *c*. 690–700 (EMC no. 1996.0063), and d) a Series C from northwest Kent, dating to *c.*700–710 (EMC no. 1998.0053); e/f) From the mid-eighth century coins more consistently carry the name of the ruler (together with that of moneyer and sometimes the town in which they were based) such as these: e) Eadberht Præn (796–798) (EMC no. 2009.0092), and f) Cuthred (798–807) (EMC no. 2009.0264)

Opposite from top

Plate 11. The linear earthwork known in AD 814 as the *Faestendic* (or 'strong dyke') in Joydens Wood on the eastern side of the Cray Valley, near Bexley. Although now heavily eroded the earthwork still remains an impressive obstacle; not one likely to stop a large-scale army, to be sure, but capable of stopping or slowing down local warbands, brigands, and others of nefarious intent! Photograph courtesy of Steve Thoroughgood

Plate 12. Aerial photograph of the excavations in 2009 of Lyminge minster by students from the universities of Reading and Kent. Clearly visible is the density of negative features such as pits, post-holes and ditches across the area, attesting to the scale of activities in the vicinity of the church. Photograph courtesy of Gabor Thomas

Plate 14. Photograph showing the relationship between St Mary-in-Castro church (left) and the Roman *pharos* (right), as well as the substantial earthwork in which they are sited. Image courtesy of Detraymond, Wikipedia Commons

Plate 15. The impressive flint walls of Eynsford castle are the remains of the early Norman fortification, built, perhaps, in the last decade of the eleventh century. It is possible that the earthwork platform the castle occupies is of a Late Anglo-Saxon stronghold, parts of which – including the base of a timber tower – were excavated in the 1950s–1970s. Other castles at Goltho (Li) and Portchester (Ha) have demonstrated similar re-use of high-status functions from the Anglo-Saxon into the Norman periods, emphasising some of the ways in which the English elite were replaced by new Norman rulers after 1066. Photograph courtesy of Malcolm Muir

that a wide network of links existed. Taking the Kentish keystone-garnet disc brooch as an example, mapping of their distribution in southern Britain sees genuine brooches appearing in Hampshire and the Isle of Wight, yet further afield we find copies and poor imitations, for example in West Wiltshire and in the cemetery at Edix Hill, Barrington, Cambridgeshire, perhaps in lieu of the genuine article, but significant enough by stylistic association. If we take the example of iron weaving-swords used as marriage gifts, then the presence of one with a child in Holywell Row grave 11 in Suffolk suggests an association of some kind between Anglian and Kentish groups.

The relationship of East Kent to West Kent was one of superiority and subordination. The options for East Kentish expansion were seemingly limited by geography. Directly to the south and west lay the dense forest of the Weald, and whilst it might be suspected that Kent had control over this tract of land, it offered no political enhancement for a power seeking elite. As a geographically small kingdom, West Kent was seemingly unable to withstand the pressure from its more powerful neighbour, seeking to control the coastal and road links with the Thames Valley. In addition, the Darenth Valley and the dip slopes of the North Downs to the west of the Medway offered some of the best and most fertile soils in southern Britain. The archaeological material from the two provinces hint that a primary East Kent kingdom annexed the province to the west from more ethnically 'Saxon' peoples during the sixth century.

In origin West Kent may have been part of the East Saxon kingdom across the Thames Estuary, united rather than divided by the river, with the first crossing point between Tilbury and Higham along the alignment of the Roman road from Rochester where it diverged from Watling Street. Certainly the site distribution in Kent west of the Medway in the sixth century shows a focus on the land abutting the Thames and the river tributaries leading up into the North Downs. The material culture of West Kent in the sixth century was clearly Saxon by type, with parallels amongst the material from Mucking in southwest Essex, particularly pottery, and the zone of Saxon settlement in the Upper Thames Valley. The distribution of the distinctive Saxon type saucer brooches emphasises this point. Typically worn as pairs of brooches, one at each shoulder, they are present with several women buried in each cemetery in West Kent. They do also occur in East Kent, more usually with a single woman and with little evidence that they could have been of Kentish manufacture.

Perhaps the bonds between the two kingdoms were also cemented by marriage in the sixth century. Conversely, there seems little evidence of East Kentish brooch styles having a presence in West Kent, with no keystone-garnet disc brooches recorded there. The dividing line between the two parts of the modern county is the River Medway. In the sixth century the cemetery at Chatham Lines, excavated by James Douglas in the mid to late eighteenth century, was strategically placed to dominate the river crossing along the Roman road at Rochester and a probable landfall on the tidal approaches. It is a classically East Kentish site, with objects probably dating to the first half of the sixth century, yet despite its proximity to West Kent, shows absolutely no influence from that area. It is therefore difficult to assess the nature of East Kentish control over West Kent and to pinpoint the period within which this control was established, other than from documentary sources of the seventh century. Perhaps importantly, the westernmost boundary of Kent with Surrey was fixed perhaps as early as the seventh century in part along the London to Lewes Roman road, with Westerham as the furthest western settlement. This may well have coincided with the western boundary of the earlier, smaller kingdom.

Identification of a strong relationship between Kent and the Isle of Wight in the sixth century is based on two sources. Bede suggests that there was a common ethnic origin for the peoples of Kent and Wight and indeed, the Roman name for Wight, Uecta, appears in the Kentish genealogy. Archaeologically speaking, the material culture of the two areas is similar from early on in the sixth century, represented by southern Scandinavian metalwork from the same points of origin. Kentish style brooches, such as the small square-headed type, are found, although it cannot be established whether we are seeing objects imported from Kent or objects made on Wight by local metalsmiths. The most significant burial was Chessell Down grave 45, that of a woman who would have been on a par with her contemporary Sarre grave 4. Unusually, she was also accompanied by an engraved, copper-alloy pail, provenanced from the eastern Mediterranean and of a type as yet not found in Kent.

The mainland opposite Wight in present day Hampshire has also been described in historical sources as 'Jutish'. The extent of this enclave ran from around the western edge of the New Forest through to Hayling Island, taking in all of the coastal plain. The cemeteries here are similar to the earliest phases of the Wight cemeteries, but have little to compare with the strong Kentish material culture of sixth-century Wight. Bede indicates that both Wight and the Jutish mainland could be considered self-governing political entities.

Religious beliefs

The period up to the arrival of the Augustinian mission to King Æthelberht in AD 597 has been characterised as 'pagan' as a counterpoint to Christianity, but what were the beliefs prevalent amongst Kentish people in the sixth century? Again, we must ask to what extent late Roman Britain was actually

Christianised. The outward signs of Christianity were familiar to the upper echelons of society, although it is entirely feasible that the monotheistic religion did not percolate fully through to the rural Romano-British population, who may have maintained their own cult practices. These may perhaps have survived as practices through the 'pagan period', but again we have no archaeological evidence for this.

Whilst there is no evidence for places of Christian worship in use in the sixth century, it is reasonable to infer that Christian people may have been present within a society where very different belief systems coexisted. Here, the probable presence of Frankish people may have brought some familiarity with their religion, particularly if Frankish brides, as evidenced by their gold-braided headdresses, were able to continue their habitual modes of worship in their new domicile. Orientation of the burial might be another indicator, but there were many variations in orientations used, including south to north with the head at the south. West to east, head to the west, was the most frequent occurrence and therefore not necessarily particularly indicative of a minority religious preference.

Can we find evidence of places of pagan worship? Margaret Gelling comments that only a few relevant place-names have been identified nationally, falling into two categories: names containing *hearg* (as in Harrow) and those containing *wēoh, wīh* (the sole Kentish example is Wye), both considered to mean 'heathern shrine'. Place-name elements might include the names of the gods *Wōden, Þunor* and *Tīw*. The charter boundary name Thunoreshlaew on the Isle of Thanet indicates a barrow linked with a god's name, whilst Woodnesborough may also be similarly associated. The nature of the 'heathen shrine' is equally difficult to establish, although Tacitus's description in *Germania* is perhaps the nearest we may get to understanding the manifestations of Germanic beliefs, albeit recorded 400 years earlier. He comments on the search for omens, the casting of lots and the role of women as holy and gifted with prophecy. Their holy places were woods and groves and at that time did not portray their gods in human likeness. This trait may however run counter to the later and very obvious depictions of a helmeted man that recurs as a motif on brooches, bracteates and re-used Roman coins on necklaces.

We can reconstruct something of their ways of thinking by looking at the kinds of objects that were deposited in furnished burials. In the region of seventy per cent of sixth-century burials had grave goods associated with them, including weapons, personal dress fittings and a restricted range of ancillary objects. Certain objects have been interpreted as having ritual and amuletic value (*Plate 8*), the majority of which accompanied women. Crystal balls, occasionally with a perforated silver spoon, hung from the belts of the richly adorned women in Bifrons graves 42, 51 and 64 and in Sarre grave 4, amongst over twenty known from Kent. The spoons may have been linked to the serving of wine in Roman culture, but their connection to the crystal balls is unknown, although an association of linked concepts must be inferred. Amber, the fiery coloured and translucent fossil resin from the southern shores of the Baltic, is the most frequently found stone in burials, primarily with women, strung as beads, although occasionally found individually with males as sword beads. Earlier documentary sources ascribe medicinal and prophylactic properties to it, underpinning its use as an amulet.

Colour, texture, sound and movement all seem to play a part in the construction of the burial tableaux, through the inclusion of cloth and clothing, organic remains such as seeds and animal bones (dog, ox, fowl, sheep, horse and lobster) and the placing of objects and receptacles around the body, all of which can be interpreted as redolent of everyday life in the present as much as a prospect of a sumptuous life in another world beyond death. The degree to which they may have differentiated between the two is unknown – in any case death was never far away, given an average age at death of between thirty and forty. It would appear that cemeteries and settlements were probably spatially linked, in that they were intervisible and in proximity to one another, so that the living were near to the dead, and that the dead were also visible within the landscape due to the siting of cemeteries in relation to routeways, for example the string of sites along the north side of the Isle of Thanet, visible to craft passing through the Wantsum Channel.

Conclusions

Kent in the first eighty years of the sixth century was a vigorous and powerful arena, with wide-sweeping changes taking place to social and economic structures. The waxing and waning of Frankish and southern Scandinavian influences, the annexation of a neighbouring territory, military adventures, perhaps beyond its borders, control of trade in elite goods and the establishment of a kingly dynasty all point to a well-organised and hierarchical society, confident in its role within the context of the post-Roman world around the North Sea and beyond. Whether at the beginning of the century the upper echelons of society thought of themselves as Jutes is debatable, but by the end they were demonstrably Kentish.

CHAPTER 4

——•——

ÆTHELBERHT'S KENT:
C.AD 589–618

Introduction: The emergence of kings

How do men come to power? This question has particular relevance for an understanding of sixth- and seventh-century England, for it is then that certain individuals emerge for the first time fully in the historical record. King Æthelberht of Kent was one such individual, and the first clearly attested English king, thanks in no small part to Bede, who records a number of significant aspects of Æthelberht's reign. Although it is not entirely clear as to his exact dates, Æthelberht is likely to have ruled from *c.*589–616/618. Under him Kent appears for the first time as a fully formed kingdom displaying many of the nascent characteristics of later medieval states, including law codes, a royal house, and functioning military, political and economic apparatus. Significantly to Bede, Æthelberht was also the first English king to be baptised, and with him Kent became, however notionally, a Christian kingdom.

The narrative of the conversion is outlined by Bede in colourful terms. The Christian mission to Kent landed in the spring of AD 597 on the Ebbsfleet peninsular near Sandwich. Under the leadership of Augustine (of whose early life little is known except that he had previously been prior of the monastery of Saint Andrew's on the Coelian hill in Rome), some forty monks arrived from Rome charged by Pope Gregory with converting the kingdoms of Anglo-Saxon England. King Æthelberht received the missionaries hospitably, and in all likelihood Kent had been picked as the starting point for the mission because Augustine had reason to believe they would be granted protection by the husband of a Christian queen. Æthelberht had married a Frankish princess, Bertha, daughter of Charibert, King of Paris, around AD 580. The mission had an early success, converting Æthelberht within a few years of its arrival, and simultaneously establishing a far-reaching programme for the organisation of the Church in England based on the metropolitan see of Canterbury.

Æthelberht's role in the conversion of England was not his only claim to fame. Bede (*HE*, II.3) also tells us that Æthelberht was a *Bretwalda* who governed all of the English people south of the Humber. Whilst it is unlikely that this Old English term is much other than a description of the relative status between kings, it seems as if Æthelberht did claim some kind of overlordship over the East Saxons and London (*HE*, II.6). In a somewhat ambiguous entry Bede describes Æthelberht's relationship with Rædwald, king of East Anglia, explaining that Rædwald retained *ducatus*, or military command of his people, even while Æthelberht held *imperium* (*HE*, II.25). At the very least, it is unlikely that a Christian mission could have been established in London in AD 604 had Æthelberht not wielded some influence over the area, nor would he have figured so prominently in Gregory the Great's plans for the conversion of Britain if he were not able to make possible the mission beyond the boundaries of his own kingdom.

That kings like Æthelberht are recorded at all is testimony to their success, but alongside them many of the institutions that supported their power also come into view in archaeological and historical sources. From these we can begin to understand some of the processes of political change that were taking place in England around AD 600, as well as the sources of power to which men like Æthelberht could lay claim. Amongst these were the coercive powers of military might and law enforcement, the ability to collect taxes and impose leadership over people, a role in the judiciary, and in the economy. Examination of these powers from the available evidence reveals a dynamic phase in the development of Kent.

Military power

Military prowess was certainly one of the routes for personal aggrandisement. Although compiled several centuries later than the events it purports to chart, the *Anglo-Saxon Chronicle* and other sources make it clear that the sixth and seventh centuries were tumultuous times in which a roll call of petty kings, chiefs and nobles waged war on one another. During the later sixth and seventh century, most of this warfare was concentrated in the west of England. The *Anglo-Saxon Chronicle* records passages of conflict between Germanic people and the native British, but in areas at a geographical distance from Kent, in present day Wiltshire around Marlborough and Salisbury, suggesting a more stable situation may have existed in the east of Britain. Nevertheless, warfare continued to be significant in Kentish affairs. The *Anglo-Saxon Chronicle* also records that in AD 568 the West Saxons fought against Æthelberht and drove his forces back into Kent, indicating expansionist tendencies by a – by then – powerful kingdom, even if we cannot take such precise dating at face value.

In such an environment demonstrated ability in warfare and leadership could secure the loyalty of warrior followers, and through them, political domination of a region. This was, in many ways, rule through fear, and different scales of violence and reprisal existed at all levels of society. Successful campaigning outside the kingdom could cement the bonds of loyalty between a king and his warband, but failure could turn those warriors against him. In terse entries the *Anglo-Saxon Chronicle* details a succession of kings and royal families, barely disguising the political betrayal, rebellion and intrigue that must have characterised these early states.

It is likely that the political geography of Kent was determined by episodes of military expansion. For much of its existence as an independent kingdom Kent appears to have been divided into two provinces each ruled by its own king. Joint kings are recorded in written documents during the seventh and eighth centuries, with the ruler of the western kingdom seemingly acting as junior partner to the dominant eastern king. This relationship may well have its roots in the political context of the sixth century. It is likely that at this time the eastern Kentish kingdom annexed areas beyond the Medway and it is these western territories that formed an area of semi-independent jurisdiction thereafter (see chapter 3). This subdivision seems also to be fossilised in the two dioceses of Canterbury and Rochester, with one or another king often associated with either community. This picture has also been sustained with the possible identification of a 'western district' (or *gē*, related to the German *Gau*) within East Kent, centred on Wester in the parish of Linton, and corresponding with the 'eastern ge' of *Easter-gē* or Eastry (*Fig. 22*). Similar amalgamations of smaller provinces by successful royal families are known from elsewhere, such as the kingdom of Northumbrians (based on the earlier provinces of Bernicia and Deira), and that of the East Angles (comprising the North and South-folk, as well as the Isle of Ely, which is named as a separate region by Bede and is also a –*gē* place-name), perhaps fossilising comparable processes of kingdom formation.

Law enforcement

Beyond warfare it is clear that violence existed also in the everyday. The threat of bloody reprisal was never far away in earlier Anglo-Saxon society, with certain forms of violence sanctioned in the earliest law codes of the seventh century. These tell us of an elaborate system of payments, connected with a notion of *leodgeld* – or *wergild*, a man's price, or bloodprice

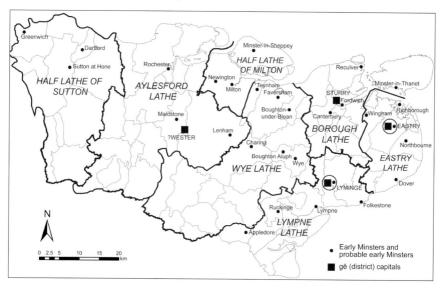

Fig. 22. The administrative geography of Kent, showing the location of possible archaic centres denoted by the place-name element *gē*; the hundreds and lathes (bold) as recorded in Domesday Book; and the location of early minsters

– through which kindred could be compensated by the initial wrongdoer for injuries gained through robberies, brawls, or fights. Should this compensation be refused, kindred had a duty to take vengeance, and disputes were often settled locally (and at times brutally) according to well-understood principles of social custom. The success of leaders lay in their ability to police and limit these forms of violence and the corrosive effect they could have on society.

The law code of Æthelberht is the earliest of written sources for Kent. It is not unique in either form or content, as it has parallels in contemporary continental pagan Germanic law, although these are known from a century earlier and were recorded in Latin. Probably first written down *c.*AD 600, Æthelberht's law code lays out a series of monetary recompenses that must be paid for certain actions. The first law is a statement about compensation for the theft of Church property – whether this was in the original order of the laws or was a later insertion we cannot be certain, nor indeed whether there were ever more than the extant ninety entries, covering other areas of royal jurisdiction. The law code has survived only as a transcription within a much later document, the *Textus Roffensis*, which was compiled by a literate monk in the early twelfth century. The *Textus* contains other legal and ecclesiastical records, mostly pertaining to the diocese of Rochester and importantly also includes the two later codes of Eadric and Wihtred. Æthelberht's law code is significant in its own right as the earliest document to be written down in the English language – no Latin version exists, but our knowledge of it has been filtered through various modernisations of the original language – historians are able to decipher several linguistic forms contained within it, suggesting cumulative transcriptions that may well have changed the sense and meaning of the original over time to fit into a different social context. Certainly, the use of Franco-Norman terminology for the social relationships of kingship might be questioned for their validity in the early seventh century.

The version offered in Appendix 1 is reproduced from Frederick Attenborough's *Laws of the Earliest English Kings*, although other translations from Old English are now available online for consultation, together with the major Anglo-Saxon dictionaries. The Attenborough version is presented to illustrate the point that translations and understandings of the meanings within the text are not fixed and are in the process of constant re-appraisal by modern scholars. One might observe that a great deal of emphasis within the laws relates to the male body, with a long sequence of compensations for a wide range of injuries to bodily parts – the most expensive being to the 'generative organ', with the cheapest being for the pulling of hair, from which we might infer that reproductive capacity was a prime component of a masculine identity, with an unblemished body and flowing locks. It appears imperative that fighting between men should be curtailed to the greatest degree, perhaps to preserve their bodies and fighting instincts for excursions beyond the bounds of Kent and its dependent territories. There is also an emphasis on property rights, including over slaves, and on inheritance. Paramount is the payment due to the king for injury to those who came under his protection or were living on one of his estates.

It is evident from these laws that kings had not yet appropriated many of the acts of government that they were later to do. Many disputes appear to have been settled without the intervention of officials. It is entirely possible that the written code was a formalisation of customs and practices that were usually transmitted orally and held as common knowledge. At the heart of these laws lay the family – in itself an extension of the king's own kin – and the family's responsibility to protect its own members. It was the duty of kin to take vengeance for injustices, and in codifying the bloodprice rewarded for different crimes, the earliest laws of Kent simply served to regulate and limit local feuding.

Social complexity around the year AD 600

From Æthelberht's law codes we might also read a range of clearly defined social statuses already in place by the beginning of the seventh century. This hierarchical system clearly articulated the role of kings at the apex of society. An individual's prestige and rank was determined by how closely they were related to the king, and it was with respect to him that one's worth was determined. These laws make it clear that there was a sharp division between freemen and slaves (a *theow* or *thrall*), with only free people enjoying the full protection of the law. They also show that there were many different ranks of free: from kings (who were worth between twelve and thirty times that of a noble), to *eorl* (well-born men with military obligations) worth 300 gold shillings to *coerls* (ordinary freemen) valued at 100 shillings, and three grades of lowly *laets* (labourers), worth from 80 to 40 shillings.

However, it is possible for the non-specialist to take the translation too much at face value and be misled as to the complexities of early Anglo-Saxon society. In early medieval poetry there exists a prevalent ideology of opportunism and warfare, suggesting a certain degree of fluidity in social classes that was qualified by rights to violence derived from age and descent, and was therefore not restricted to the elite. A further case in point is the status of women and this issue, as indicated by these and other law codes, has been subject to revision through new translations. It is possible to suggest that the Anglo-Saxon laws show women having a degree of freedom in marrying and in determining the course of their lives after marriage, particularly in widowhood. It is significant to note that by the ninth century, gender roles are bi-laterally defined around the male 'spear' side and the female 'spindle' side, although the role of women as craft producers is not readily apparent from the documentary sources. Some scholars go as far as to suggest that the legal status of women improved between the seventh and tenth centuries, although in direct contrast Christine Fell charts a decline from the seventh through to the twelfth centuries from a golden age of power, wealth and culture to one of post-Conquest chatteldom. Fell re-examined the meaning of 'friwif locbor' in chapter 73 of the Laws, translated by Attenborough as a 'freeborn woman with flowing locks', and considers a more accurate interpretation to be relating to a freewoman with responsibility for the carrying of keys, one that resonates with the archaeological evidence from furnished burial for the sixth and seventh centuries in Kent and elsewhere in lowland Britain. Keys played a significant part in the construction of the image of the 'lady of the house' in the Germanic world and later written sources attest to wedding ceremonies wherein sets of keys denote a woman attaining responsibility for valuables, perhaps held in a locked container or room. Keys, either singles or groups attached to the chatelaine at the left waist of an interred female, are a recurrent feature of early Anglo-Saxon burial, particularly evident in Kent where ironwork formed a much larger component of the burial assemblage than elsewhere.

Is it possible to align the early Kentish law codes with contemporary archaeological evidence? As one might expect, the archaeology is informing us about other changes and processes which cannot be readily interpreted through the prism of the unique documentary sources. The character of the archaeological evidence for the period AD 595–650 is very different from that of the fifth and sixth centuries, and it is now possible to assert that the phase AD 575–625 was in many ways transitional within the broader temporal context, generally termed as the Final Phase of furnished burial, framed from AD 570 to the end of the seventh century. The key features are a change and diminution in the repertoire of artefacts deposited in furnished burial and a visible shift towards cultural uniformity, particularly in the spheres of dress styles and art. John Hines, in his discussion of cultural identity and archaeology in Britain after Rome, proposes that conformity was a 'pervasive trend' in Anglo-Saxon and Germanic culture, resulting in a 'rudimentary form of Anglo-Saxon imperialism' in the sixth and seventh centuries, that seemingly had no appreciation or room for the cultural diversity that characterised the furnished burials of the sixth century. Perhaps we can see a place here for the very detailed and prescriptive law codes of Æthelberht.

There are two major characteristics of the Final Phase of furnished burial: an abrupt end to artefacts exhibiting Style I decoration and the flourishing of those with Style II; and the pervasive tendency towards greater funerary display by a minority elite and a decrease for the majority. Style II is in great evidence in Kent, Anglia and Mercia, and is found as the decorative format for a restricted range of types of objects, although there are considerable numbers of these, some of which are the most famous artefacts from the early Anglo-Saxon period. Although essentially still based on animal shapes, Style II is more formalised and restricted than Style I, with, visible to the practiced eye, a regular use of conventions, for example confronted or opposed animal shapes placed to form symmetrical motifs in harmonious rhythm. Through the use of correspondence analysis of the stylistic components, Karen Høilund Nielsen has established that there are two probable sources for this style in England: Scandinavia for the Anglian objects, including those from Sutton Hoo mound 1 and introduced there sometime after AD 550; and the Continent for the Kentish objects, but not earlier than AD 565.

Elite burial

The Final Phase of furnished burial provides good indications that Anglo-Saxon society became increasingly polarised around the period of Æthelberht's reign. Not only in Kent but throughout England, in the decades either side of AD 600, the phenomenon of distinctive elite burials begins to appear, as an explicit means of expressing status and dynastic power. Special structures might be used to define the grave within the cemetery, such as ditches or chambers, which may have been part of spatially separate kin groupings. Also, we see the appearance of isolated burials on a grand scale, not connected to everyday cemeteries, but forming prominent landscape markers in their own right. Kent has provided no burial comparable to that of Sutton Hoo mound 1 or the more recently excavated chamber grave at Prittlewell, Essex, both dated to after AD 625. That is not to suggest, however, that the wealth of Kent had dissipated by this time, as we have yet to identify the potentially sumptuous burial place of Æthelberht and Queen Bertha (Bede places them in the chapel of St Martin, within the monastery of St Peter and St Paul at Canterbury and, as Christians, they may well have opted for burial without grave goods) and we do have evidence elsewhere of Kentish hierarchy in the form of the male inhumation at Taplow, Buckinghamshire. Indeed, if we see women in a subordinate position throughout this period, then another explanation is required for the richly furnished female burials of the first quarter of the seventh century. So, let us consider the burial remains of a selected group: the man from Taplow; a woman discovered at Sarre in 1860; a woman in the barrow cemetery at Kingston; a possible cremation burial from Coombe Woodnesborough; and a group of men buried with weapons, including the owner of the unique 'Finglesham Man' buckle (*Fig. 23*).

The cemetery at Sarre on the Isle of Thanet has proved to be both extensive and long-lived, with over 320 individuals buried between AD 480 and 700. The first discovery was in 1843 when a grave was accidentally uncovered in the field above the – by then in-filled – Wantsum Channel, containing a bronze bowl with vandyked rim and a gold and garnet brooch with star design. In 1860, workmen digging a pit for the steam engine at Sarre windmill found, six feet below the surface, another gold and garnet brooch, and a bronze bowl similar to the first, together with a host of other objects. Unfortunately, the circumstances of discovery precluded proper recording and grave planning, although it was noted that the skeleton lay with the head to the northwest. More fortunately, the finds were acquired by the British Museum, where the archive was accessioned in tiny handwriting within the leather-bound registers and comprises: a composite jewelled disc brooch, from on the 'left breast'; two keys and a copper-alloy ring; a neck-lace of two amethysts; six glass and eleven amber beads; four gold coins and a millefiori glass pendant; an iron buckle loop; a copper-alloy pin; unidenti-fied iron artefacts, including a possible iron sheath guard, a pursemount or firesteel; and two knives, both with fragments of a leather sheath. The bronze bowl was an imported object from the eastern Mediterranean that had been damaged and repaired. The museum has retained the organic contents of the bowl, which included a leather pouch with a fringe or tassel, a wooden bowl of beech or maple, burnt animal bone lying on a wad of cloth, oyster shell, stems and seeds or hips of a plant, perhaps hawthorn, hazelnuts, pads of textile and a layer of grass or rush stems from underneath the wooden bowl. A large sword was also noted (since lost or decayed in the museum), possibly a weaving beater or a weapon – the possibility that this may have been a double female/male inhumation cannot now be verified. The gold necklace coins were of the eastern emperors, Mauricius and Heraclius (AD 582–602; 610–41) and of Clothar II of France (613–28), thus giving a date of deposi-tion of probably AD 620 or later. Sarre (1860) and the earlier discovered grave represent the last display of rich female burials in this part of Kent.

However, near contemporaries were being buried elsewhere, notably in the new and extensive barrow cemeteries that flourished on the downlands of East Kent, with wealth of a comparable nature. The Kingston barrow inhumation cemetery, on the western side of Barham or Kingston Downs, was excavated 1767–1773 by the Reverend Bryan Faussett and by Thomas Wright in the nineteenth century. Of the 308 graves opened, 183 contained remains of wooden coffins. All but forty-five graves were marked by small mounds, and with fourteen exceptions, all were buried with the head to the west. Although many barrows contained little more than a skeleton with a knife and belt buckle, grave 205, a double female inhumation, contained the now famous Kingston brooch, another composite jewelled disc brooch in Style II. The largest of the seventh-century brooches of this type, it is unique in the quality of its craftsmanship, displaying gold, garnet, blue glass and shell within a series of radiating cloisonné cells and is clearly of Kentish style and manufacture. Grave 205, and her sister burial in grave 299 with a jewel-plated disc brooch, dated to the first half of the seventh century, represent the begin-nings of important new communities in new locations as the Anglo-Saxon settlement expanded away from the coastal areas in the late sixth and seventh centuries. The landscape and settlement evidence for the early Anglo-Saxon period appears to suggest a significant role for sheep in the agrarian economy. This is particularly evidenced by the incidence of sheiling field names on the North Downs, with these possibly becoming farmstead sites when the

Downs were more permanently settled from the seventh century onwards. It is with these secondary settlements that the large barrow cemeteries, notably at Kingston Down and Sibertswold-Barfreston, are associated.

Outside of Kent, the late sixth- or early seventh-century burial from the mound at Taplow has prompted discussion on the strategic importance of Kentish hegemony over the productive Upper Thames Valley, coincident with control of London. The large burial mound, 24.4m in diameter when excavated in 1883, is still visible as a garden landscaped feature within the grounds of Taplow Court, itself within a prehistoric earthwork complex, sited on a remote plateau to command passage up and down the adjacent river. Second only to Sutton Hoo in wealth and display – including personal adornment, military hardware and feasting equipment with nineteen vessels, most notable the range of silver gilt drinking horns and a rare lyre – the male buried here is deemed to have been a Kentish 'prince' by virtue of the sheer quality and point of origin of his material culture that stood in stark contrast to the surrounding milieu of Saxon culture within which he found himself.

The issue of the extent to which the earlier, Scandinavian practice of covering the whole contents of a grave with a light cloak or blanket continued into the early Anglo-Saxon period is indeterminable, given the variability in textile preservation and recording. Notable in the late sixth to early seventh centuries is a widespread incidence of cloths being used to cover the mouths of metal receptacles, such as metal-bound wooden buckets and copper-alloy bowls. Examples include the bronze cremation bowl in Sutton Hoo mound 4 and a bronze bowl from Coombe, Woodnesborough, Kent – the Coombe broken diamond twill z/s is comparable to that from the high status burial at Broomfield, Essex – both of these latter examples using Scandinavian type closing borders. The burial at Coombe, in the parish of Woodnesborough on the southern edge of the Wantsum Channel, is another of the great Kentish burials of the late sixth/early seventh centuries for which we have frustratingly insufficient detail regarding its location, form and content. From antiquarian records and contemporary accounts from the eighteenth century it appears that dispersed around the current church may have been a mixed rite cemetery – references are made to layers of calcined bone and a cache of thirty glass vessels. A single burial, dug into in 1845 by a Suffolk-based amateur collector of antiquities reputedly produced the copper-alloy bowl with 'a veil of cloth … in the exact position it was placed by the affectionate hand of the mourning relative' and two swords, a spearhead, beads and a pendant – altogether an exceptionally interesting group of finds. The human calcined bone in the bowl is indicative of the cremation of a high status male in the late sixth century – a rare event.

The most unique object from this period is the so-called 'Finglesham Man' buckle (*Fig. 23*). Dated to the second quarter of the seventh century, this object was excavated from the burial of a male, aged approximately eighteen years at death. Whilst in form, with a triangular plate and shield on the buckle tongue, it appears as a normal high status object, yet the motif is extraordinary. Depictions of the human form are rare within early Anglo-Saxon culture, yet here we have a crude figure of a naked man, wielding a spear in each hand and wearing a double horned helmet, the whole cast in copper alloy and gilded with gold. Parallels to this image can be found on contemporary Swedish objects – the dies from Torslunda, Őland and on the Valsgärde grave 8 helmet. The image has affinities with the clothed horned dancers on the Sutton Hoo mound 1 helmet plates. The presence of this archaic form of heathen iconography speaks of ongoing contacts with the Scandinavian world, but ones other than the probable homelands of the fifth and sixth century settlers. The conversion to Christianity had already begun in Kent, but here images and meanings of a pagan past and contacts with powerful pagan neighbours still had currency.

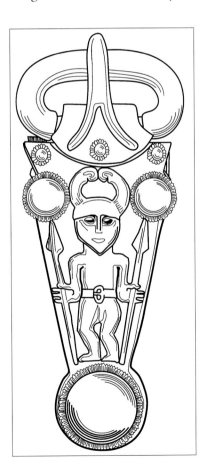

Fig. 23. The Finglesham buckle

A place for leaders

It was not only the emerging elite who were concerned with demonstrating their position in society. Although it is first recorded by Bede, it is likely that it was in Æthelberht's reign that the Kentish royal genealogy was first drafted. Not only does this list the name of Æthelberht's father, Eormenric, whose reign would have coincided with the main period of Frankish cultural influence in Kent (see chapter 3), it details the ancestry of the Kentish royal house stretching further back to Hengist and Horsa, the first 'Saxons' to arrive in England, and beyond them ultimate descent from the Germanic war god, Woden. On this basis Æthelberht appears to have claimed divine right of rule, or at the very least, an unassailable pedigree. Furthermore, the royal genealogy makes clear that the House of Æthelberht was regarded synonymously with the 'people of Kent'. Bede, probably following an oral tradition rather than contemporary documentary sources, traces Eormenric's ancestry thus:

> Eormenric, son of Octa, and after his grandfather Œric, surnamed Oisc, the kings of the Kentish folk are commonly known as *Oiscings*.

Alongside this genealogy it appears as if Christianity itself played an important role in underscoring Æthelberht's place in history. At the very least the Christian Church, through Bede and others, helped commemorate Æthelberht's life and death; his place of burial under the *porticus* of St Martin within the monastery of St Peter and St Paul is still marked with a plaque. But the Church also helped to propagate an idealised model of society in which kings, as heavenly-sanctified leaders, were granted a crucial and central place in society, with attendant responsibilities of rule.

Some of these roles can be inferred archaeologically. In many cases kings could only arbitrate on points of custom in local disputes in person. This was one of the reasons that kings did not have a permanent capital, but spent their reigns perpetually patrolling their kingdoms, for it meant they could physically impose their will over their subjects. But this constant life-on-the move also had other functions: frequent gatherings together of subjects in semi-ritualised settings enhanced the status of kings. They might demonstrate their position in society by wearing a crown, or other obvious symbols of rank and status. Examples of the kinds of kingly objects that might have been used have been discovered from the burial of Sutton Hoo mound 1 and include a whetstone resembling a sceptre and an iron stand that may have been used as a flaming standard, that finds parallels also in an object from a high-status burial at Benty Grange, Derbyshire.

In this way, particularly before the creation of fully functioning bureaucratic systems – which only really began to emerge after the ninth century – kings were the glue of society. As the heads of extended kinship groups kings linked communities together in both conceptual and physical terms. Perhaps the clearest aspect of this role was in the control of wealth and economic exchange that provided kings with one of their main sources of political power. Their position was maintained by collection of subsistence goods from their dependents and the flow of wealth downwards from king to subjects. By moving around their kingdom kings collected subsistence goods directly from their source; a particularly important function during the periods of the fifth to seventh centuries when there was no coined money but one which continued well into the Norman period. Tax was food, and food perished. So it was only through peripatetic kingship that the loyalty of subjects could be constantly reiterated through public consumption and feasting. In this sense kings were essential in linking communities together, as they were the point through which all goods were redistributed. Before the emergence of markets it was via kings that fishermen got arable staple, and farmers got fish, if not physically through them, then through their network of local retainers.

These transactions often took the form of reciprocal gift exchange – a system well documented in ethnographical studies. From these we know that gifting was a complex form of exchange that transcended monetary considerations. It was a gesture and a bond, imposing obligations on both parties, especially for the recipient, and was matched by counter-gifts. In this way gifting was a method of social cohesion, for it created relationships in time. In return for productive goods or objects of luxurious wealth, kings would receive the loyalty of their subjects. Often these objects also signified one's position in a chain of relationships – so-called ring-swords, swords with moulded rings on the pommel, may once have been gifts demonstrating a warrior's fealty to their lord. We have evidence of the importance of this type of ritualised gift-giving particularly in the heroic poetry of *Beowulf*, in which contrasting forms of ceremonial gift exchange are used to represent the relationships between different people. So, for example, the relationship between kings and their warrior followers were signified by gifts of arms and treasure, whilst people as a whole were more likely to receive contributions to pyre and grave goods. These objects helped constitute one as a person – *Beowulf* for example talks of an individual known as Shield-Sheafson – and it is for this reason that it was appropriate for objects to accompany one in burial.

North Sea trade and the Kentish emporia

Such wealth objects needed to be constantly regenerated. Warfare and the booty this could provide was one method; trade was the other. Through the late sixth and seventh centuries there emerged around the North Sea a range of new sites apparently designed to facilitate international trade (*Fig. 24*). These trading sites are usually referred to as 'wics' from the Old English *wic* (pronounced weech) – a place-name element for 'specialised sites' – or emporia, and include important settlements such as Ipswich, *Hamwih* (Saxon Southampton), *Lundenwic* (the trading settlement of London) and *Eoforwic* (York). The role of these emporia has commonly been interpreted in quite functional terms as the mechanism through which kings could ensure the supply of gifts to secure political stability, and a means through which they could increasingly access and monopolise their exchange and distribution. In this view, kings deliberately created these special trading sites as a way of participating in the revival of trade along the North and Baltic Sea coasts. There existed a clear link between a royal centre and its dependent industrial and exchange centre, as revenues from the latter were intimately tied to effective rulership.

Much of this argument depends on archaeological evidence from outside Kent, where excavations of these sites have revealed a number of common characteristics. Two are particularly relevant. Firstly, that all of the major kingdoms around the North Sea seem to have had a trading emporia: *Hamwih* was the market for West Saxon kings, York for the Northumbrians, Ipswich for the East Saxons, and across the Channel Quentovic (near Boulogne) for the Franks, Dorestad and Domburg at the Rhine mouths for the Frisians. So where was the emporium of the Kentish kings? Secondly, there is evidence from excavated emporia that these sites rapidly expanded in size and function from quite modest beginnings during the later seventh century as part of a general upsurge in international trading. Significantly this expansion appears to have been carried out very quickly and carefully under central (royal?) authority – the sites have evidence for regular street plans, house plots, and a concentration of craft activities – perhaps following an existing settlement model. In the case of *Hamwih* it is often thought that the emporium was developed by King Ine following his conquest of the Isle of Wight, and was designed to access the lucrative cross-Channel monopolies of trade.

Given this pattern, several studies have argued that earlier comparable developments must have existed in Kent though the settlements themselves have as yet not been identified precisely. The density of imported goods in Anglo-Saxon cemeteries in this area and some evidence of Kentish-Frankish

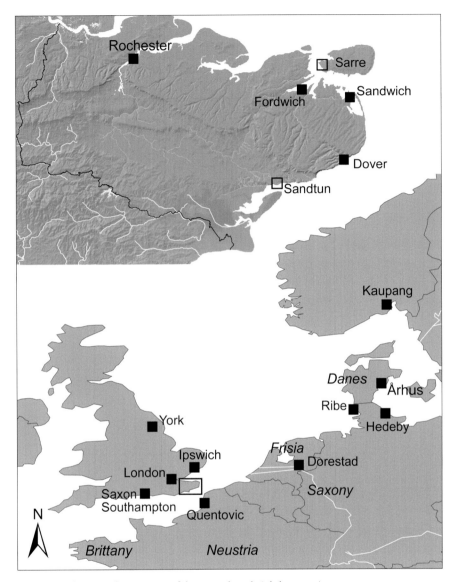

Fig. 24. North Sea trading centres of the seventh and eighth centuries

connections from both archaeological and historical sources, have been argued to represent an embryonic trading system existing from the late fifth century which later diffused throughout the country to include the other excavated sites. Documentary evidence from the seventh and eighth centuries has identified Fordwich (*Fig. 25*), Sandwich, Dover and Sarre as likely comparable trading sites which may have functioned as prototypes for the developments witnessed in other areas, and their existence is evidenced

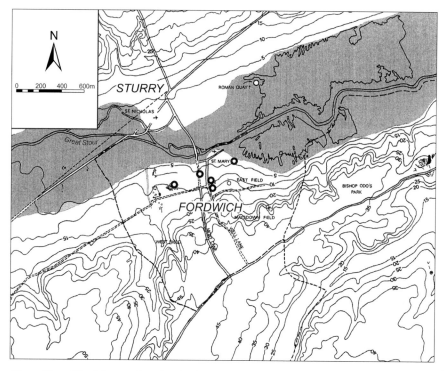

Fig. 25. Plan of the Liberty of Fordwich, showing the extent of alluvial deposits (shaded). Cropmarks are known from the west of the town centre. Shown also are probably early streets and find-spots of Anglo-Saxon date (circles)

by continued documentary allusions well into the ninth century and beyond. However, the fragmentary archaeological evidence from these sites only partially matches the picture we know of from elsewhere.

Certainly, as with other known emporia, all of the Kentish sites were economically placed, often at the hub of inland routes and waterways. Of particular importance was the Wantsum Channel – a former waterway separating the Isle of Thanet from mainland Kent – which appears on the basis of place-names, archaeological evidence and documentary sources to have been the principal shipping lane from the Dover–Deal coast into the Thames estuary and up the eastern seaboard, as it enabled maritime traffic to avoid the dangerous waters around the North Foreland headland. Significantly, from burials dating from the sixth century along this route have been recovered a number of clinker-built boat fragments, as well as fastenings, such as clench-nails and roves, lending some archaeological weight to the arguments for Kentish naval prowess.

The importance of this waterway is also substantiated by written sources. A group of eighth-century royal charters attest to vessels utilising the ports of Minster-in-Thanet and Fordwich, both of which are located on the Wantsum Channel. Furthermore, the distribution of the Old English place-name element *ōra* can also be cited to support the identification of routes of movement. Possibly derived from the Latin word meaning 'shore', *ōra* commonly refers to a flat-topped hill with a shoulder at one or both ends, but may carry a specialised sense as 'firm foreshore or gravelly landing-place'. The distribution of place-names containing the element *ōra* has a clear coincidence with both maritime and terrestrial routeways. They are known from likely landing-places and from areas beside Roman routes and appear to have been designated to mark specific topographical orientation points. In Kent, *ōra* place-names such as *Oar Farm* and *Stonar* conspicuously lie at the north and south entrances of the Wantsum Channel respectively, and may indicate the named referencing of this major maritime routeway, possibly in keeping with the codification of landmarks by medieval mariners.

At other sites, such as *Lundenwic* and *Hamwih*, the location of the emporia appears to have been governed by the local topography, with a preference for beaches on which to land the keel-less boats of the period. In London, the 'Strand' (from the Old English for 'beach') at the Aldwych (Old English for 'the old *wic*') was the centre of a large trading emporium. A similar setting appears to be suggested by the place-name Sandwich. Earlier Anglo-Saxon Sandwich – as the name suggests – appears to have been located on a sandbar to the east of the present town centre, exploiting the natural lagoon created at the mouth of the Wantsum Channel by Deal spit (*Fig. 26*). Only later, perhaps in the ninth century, was Sandwich re-sited to its present location on more solid Brickearth, much as the emporium of *Lundenwic* was moved back within the Roman city walls by Alfred the Great. Similarly at Dover specialised trading and marketing appears to have been focussed at the mouth of the River Dour adjacent to further settlements within the Roman Saxon shore fort to the west and Dover Castle to the east.

Also like other known emporia, those of Kent have evidence for clustered concentrations of continental artefacts, although in the Kentish example these tend to come from cemeteries located nearby rather than the settlements themselves. The long-lived cemeteries of Sarre and Buckland, Dover as discussed in chapter 3, have considerable evidence for Continental contacts, in addition to an unusually high proportion of weapon-bearing males, who may have represented a military establishment charged with policing trade. The concentration of Frankish fashion items at these places can be read in at least three ways (though these are by no means

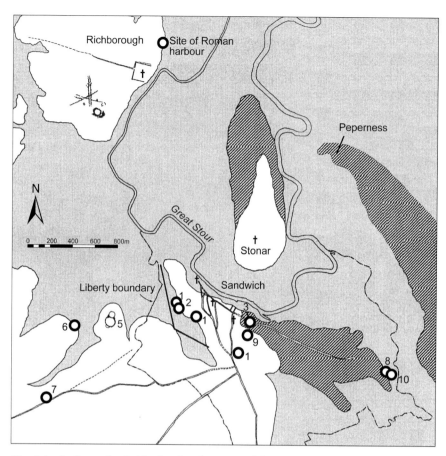

Fig. 26. Anglo-Saxon Sandwich, showing the extent of the Wantsum Channel in the Middle Anglo-Saxon period (shaded). Sand and shingle deposits are hatched. Circles show the extent of archaeological interventions up to 2000, but only numbers 6 and 10 have revealed any evidence datable to the Anglo-Saxon period, the implication being that early medieval Sandwich is likely to be located on the largely unexplored sand spur to the east of the modern town (i.e. near numbers 8 and 10)

mutually-exclusive): they might reflect the direction of luxury exchange, and crossroad settlements such as Sarre or Buckland, Dover simply occupied a monopoly in such goods; local communities deliberately assumed Continental fashions as a product of their interactions with Frankish traders; or these communities were direct clients of the Frankish state.

In other ways, however, the putative emporia of Kent differed from *wics* elsewhere. Unlike *Lundenwic* or *Hamwih*, there is little to suggest the Kentish emporia were larger than contemporary rural settlements. Fieldwork at Fordwich and Sarre has indicated that the limit of these settlements was far smaller than the 50–60ha covered by *Lundenwic* or *Hamwih* in their largest incarnations. Nor do these sites appear to be exclusive entrepôts. In contrast to the evolution of *Hamwih*, which could be envisaged as an active articulation of royal power, emporia foundations in Kent appear not to be concentrating traffic at a single site. The proliferation of at least three, possibly contemporary, taxable settlements operating from the mid-seventh century at the latest within the Wantsum Channel suggests that the sites were initially autonomous from exclusive royal policy. Rather than overt predatory kingship attempting to strategically control all aspects of trade and production, as can be argued for Ine of Wessex and *Hamwih*, Kentish royal interests encouraged the economy with only weak infrastructural support.

This raises an important point. A further characteristic, much more difficult to prove, but implicit in the whole relationship between these settlements and kingship, are kings themselves. In London, a recent re-evaluation by Robert Cowie of material excavated in the 1960s has suggested the possible location of a Middle Anglo-Saxon palace close to the riverbank at the Treasury in Whitehall, outside the area occupied by the trading settlement of *Lundenwic*. The main features included a boundary ditch, a few pits, a SFB and the remains of two successive timber halls. Significantly the width of these buildings – at 8m – is much wider than most excavated hall buildings in contemporary *Lundenwic*, perhaps suggesting royal or at least noble status. A similar spatial arrangement is suggested at Fordwich, which is located on the opposite Stour bank to Sturry (*Stūr-gē*, the Stour district captial), and also at Sandwich, which is only 4.5km from Eastry (*Easter-gē*, the eastern district capital), both of which may have been the administrative centres for large territories.

This pattern of settlement is in fact characteristic of many Middle Anglo-Saxon landscapes, in which sites of different functions were spread throughout a locale, but together comprised state-like institutions (*Fig. 27*). In the London area at least, three sites co-existed in the early seventh century: *Lundenwic*, the Treasury site, and the early ecclesiastical foundation inside the still standing Roman City walls. Similarly, Middle Anglo-Saxon Canterbury comprised the Cathedral foundation inside *Durovernum Cantiacorum*, the monastic community of St Augustine's outside the city walls, the church of St Martin's, the trading settlement of Fordwich and a putative royal villa at Sturry. The danger highlighted by this example is that our understanding of Anglo-Saxon society cannot be viewed simply from one class of settlement. Clearly this dispersed landscape of settlement is evidence for complex social organisation, even if individually, sites may appear at times to be fairly unimpressive. Archaeologically this type of organisation is called a heterarchy, a form of organisation resembling a network, rather than a hierarchy of sites,

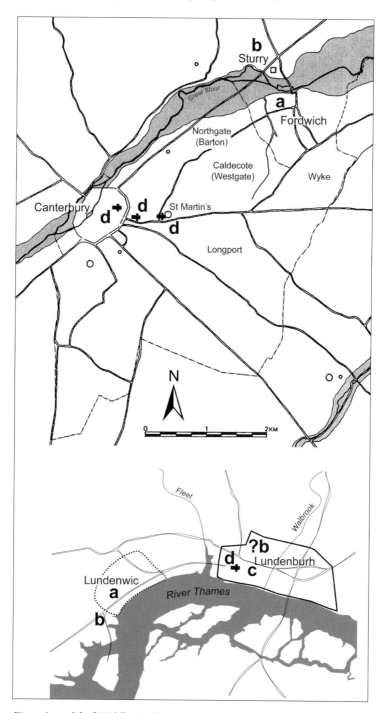

Fig. 27. A model of Middle Anglo-Saxon dispersed towns. In the seventh century the environs of both Canterbury and London displayed a range of discrete functions spread over an 'urbanised' landscape: a) market, b) royal villa, c) public assembly, d) religious houses

a form of organisation resembling a pyramid. In other archaeological cases of heterarchies – Meso-America, Inca, the British pre-Roman Iron Age – heterarchies were similarly based on a division of functions, but evolved through time to form the basis of a hierarchy of settlement. In Kent this transition only took place slowly over the course of the seventh to ninth centuries, and is examined further in the next chapter.

Royal or private initiatives?

Current work suggests that several different forms of *wic*-site existed in East Kent, providing a corollary to the more commonly discussed sites of Saxon Southampton, London, Ipswich and York. Much like these better-known examples, the sites of Fordwich and Dover can be viewed as one element in a network of settlements displaying dispersed functions. Fordwich, to the northeast of Canterbury, may have operated as the seaport for a number of settlements strung out along the Stour valley, including the ecclesiastical centres of St Martin's, St Augustine's and Christ Church, as well as the manors of Northgate, Longport, Caldecote and Sturry. Similarly Middle Anglo-Saxon Dover comprised several separate sites around the Dour mouth. This pattern contrasts with other sites such as Sarre, Sandwich and Sandtun, where evidence for continental trade and maritime activities cannot be seen as part of a heterarchy of settlements, but rather coastal communities periodically engaging in inter-regional trade.

The location and character, particularly of eastern Kentish cemeteries, suggest that many communities may have had access to a supplementary maritime economy. Certainly, if Bede is to be believed, the close political relations between the kingdom of Kent and the Isle of Wight could only have been realised through maritime connections, and it may not be too fanciful to imagine ancestors of the later medieval Cinque Ports confederacy profiting from fishing, piracy and trade with their Frankish, Frisian and Saxon neighbours from as early as the sixth and seventh centuries. Clearest evidence for this idea is offered by excavations at Sandtun, located on sand dunes on a tidal inlet hard by the Saxon shore fort of Lympne. This site has been subject to a number of excavations in 1947–8 and 1993, and evidence points to long, probably seasonal, occupation through two distinct phases covering most of the eighth and ninth centuries. A large number of finds were recovered from the occupation layers including hearths, fish-hooks, shears, scamas-axes, copper-alloy pins and fish and animal bones in large quantity, in addition to a late eighth-/early ninth-century Frankish pottery vessel. The more recent excavations revealed further large quantities of continental ceramics, in addition to evidence for fishing, textile and leather working. In all likelihood the settlement of Sandtun represents a landing place for a range of maritime activities, including fishing, trading and craft production. To this may be added salt panning, attested in written sources of AD 732 and 833 to have taken place in or near Sandtun.

From the available archaeological evidence it is probable that eastern Kent formed an area where incipient commercial activities became commonplace through the sixth and seventh centuries. Perhaps unlike the West Saxon kingdom, where international trade appears to have been initially instigated and was heavily regulated by state organisation, Kentish kings seem to have been trying to catch up and cash in on changing economic fortunes by investing in the trading infrastructure. As part of this trend it may have been during Æthelberht's reign that coins first began to be minted in England. These were primarily gold coins, known as tremisses or shillings, weighing *c.*20g, similar to contemporary coins in Francia (*Plate 13*). None bear Æthelberht's name and were minted only in small numbers, so it is unclear to what extent these coins played a monetary role rather than an ornamental or ceremonial one. Only over the course of the later seventh century did a smaller denomination coinage in silver circulate in far greater numbers marking the transition to a more fully operational cash economy (see chapter 5). As with the emporia foundations themselves, the impression gained from this development is that coinage was a measure aimed at controlling and maintaining an existing system, the prime motor of which may well have been the activities of a Kentish, Frankish, and Frisian mercantile community operating largely outside of royal control.

A Kentish people?

As part of these changes taking place during Æthelberht's reign perhaps the most significant is demonstrated in the most everyday – and personal – of material culture: dress. From the seventh century onwards, distinctive regional dress codes disappear from the archaeological record. In part this may be attributed to the decreasing incidence of burial with grave goods from which to deduce styles and possibly to an increased use of shrouds in Christian style burials. Nevertheless, iconographic and documentary sources indicate dress elements that would have required more sophisticated skills to make. Women may have had open fronted cloaks, no longer requiring front fastening brooches, that were hooded and with a more tailored shaping around the shoulders. A woollen tunic with decorated edgings was probably worn with a linen undergarment. For men, the changes appear to have been an improvement in quality, with a sleeved tunic over a linen shirt, more closely fitting trousers and gartering to the lower legs. That there were more variations in cloak styles is also probable.

Documentary sources discussing ecclesiastical dress of the seventh and eighth centuries comment on the lack of ascetic uniform and the continued use of worldly dress codes, whilst offering insight into the activities taking place within religious settlements. The Council of *Clofeshoh*, in AD 747, stated that nuns 'should undertake occupations more suitable than making fine garments'. The Venerable Bede, writing in AD 731, noted, at the monastery of nuns at Coldingham, Northumberland, that 'when they have leisure, even the nuns vowed to God abandon the propriety of their calling and spend their time weaving fine clothes'. Aldhelm wrote, *c.*AD 690–710, a tract on moral virginity dedicated to the nuns at Barking Abbey, Essex (founded AD 666), criticising elaborate dress codes found in religious houses that included fine linen shirts, scarlet tunics, silk embroidered sleeves and brightly coloured head-dresses. Certainly, the women in English religious houses were later noted for their skills in ecclesiastical embroidery, as exemplified by the gold decorated vestments associated with the shrine of Saint Cuthbert dating to *c.*AD 934. More significantly, it has been suggested that Anglo-Saxon women were actually weaving silk by the late eighth century. The appropriation of prestigious raw materials for personal use may have been a widespread and temporally enduring practice within early Christian convents.

The Church may have been further instrumental in promulgating the emergence of a common culture of 'Kentish-ness'. Hall (1989) believes that Latin Christendom provided the necessary cultural shell in which commercialism and statehood could develop. The importance of the Augustinian mission lay, not only in establishing the cultural chain, binding Kent with Francia and beyond into a larger Christian civilisation, but brought England membership within the pan-European network of culture, trade and ideas.

In the material culture of the seventh century we see evidence for these connections in the range of objects and raw materials now found in the burials. The heavy bronze Coptic bowls from the eastern Mediterranean, cowrie shells from India, Frankish wheel-thrown pots and amethysts from southern Europe are the more obvious examples, although textiles and other organic artefacts would also have been involved. From the point of view of trade, membership of a larger Christian civilisation enabled people to more freely identify with one another's culture, with the rapid spread of commercial connections the result. Although the full effects of these developments still lay in the future, the foundations for these changes had been laid by Æthelberht (and his kin).

Conclusions

Why do we remember King Æthelberht of Kent? Without Bede it is unlikely that he would have stood out particularly from the various other kings that are known to have ruled around AD 600, for all of these men played an important part in the changing shape of English society. In Æthelberht's Kent, as in other territories around the country, we have seen all the ingredients in place to support the changing character of kingship and the state. We have evidence of international contacts and specialised trade, that is to say the widening reach and diversification of royal income; we have the evidence of ideological and economic tools such as Christianity and long-distance trade goods; and we have evidence to suggest that kings were strengthening their grip over people themselves, with the introduction of money (i.e. controlled forms of exchange), laws, and religious persuasion. Yet in all of these areas, Æthelberht appears to have been a particularly skilful and innovative leader. When he died in around 616/618, none of the Kentish kings that followed would ever wield powers as significant and wide-reaching again.

CHAPTER 5

THE MIDDLE ANGLO-SAXON KINGDOM OF KENT
C.AD 650–850

Introduction: The changing map of Anglo-Saxon England

During the Middle Anglo-Saxon period (*c.*AD 650–850), the consolidation of many English kingdoms into larger more powerful units increasingly brought kings into political conflict and warfare. In some cases, smaller, weaker kingdoms were swallowed up by more powerful neighbours; in other cases, influential kings managed to establish overlordship over subordinate territories. In the latter case, underkings were expected to acknowledge their inferiority and pay tribute to their overlord, and perhaps cede important rights and institutions. Although Æthelberht had been overking of southern England, during the seventh century powerful military leaders emerged, particularly amongst the Mercians and Northumbrians, who began to dominate the wider English political landscape, eclipsing all of the Kentish kings after Æthelberht, and reducing the kingdom of Kent to a still influential, but essentially second-tier, province.

This process may already have started in Æthelberht's reign. Bede tells us that Rædwald, king of the East Angles, assumed the title of *Bretwalda* even before Æthelberht's death (*HE*, II.5). Nevertheless, Kentish kings continued to wield considerable power over their neighbours in London and Surrey for some time longer. As late as the 680s, a Kentish royal hall and a royal reeve were still present in *Lundenwic*, presumably to protect Kentish trading interests in the emporium, even if this post may by this stage have been increasingly untenable. *Lundenwic* may already have passed into Mercian hands as early as 658, and certainly by the late 680s was firmly a Mercian trading post. Significantly, it is precisely at this time that *Lundenwic* rapidly expanded in size and complexity, perhaps reflecting its new status as the premier Mercian emporium on the east coast, rather than merely one of a network of Kentish emporia. Kentish power was further threatened militarily. In AD 676, Bede records that Æthelred I of the Mercians devastated Kent, recording in horror how his 'wicked soldiery' destroyed lesser churches as well as the cathedral at Rochester (*HE*, IV.12 and V.24). This event signified the start of a period of over a hundred years when the expansion of Mercian rule into large parts of central and southern England dominated the politics of Kent.

In part, this expansion was through force of arms, but these were not large marauding armies. Seventh- and eighth-century wars in Anglo-Saxon England were fundamentally in order to gain plunder and tribute and were usually undertaken by small armies made up of the wealthy military elite and their levies. Raids into neighbouring territories gained profit, enhanced reputations and contributed to social position. Battles were accordingly short, brutal and mainly aristocratic affairs. That is not to say that they could not have considerable political repercussions, and for local kings and their followers such wars constituted a major threat that could determine the success or failure of royal dynasties.

The political scene of southern England is graphically illustrated by a document commonly referred to as the 'Tribal Hidage'. In all likelihood dating to *c*.635–80, the Tribal Hidage presents a snap-shot of the political geography of England at a point when numerous independent kingdoms still existed, but were in the process of being absorbed, conquered and overawed by more powerful neighbours (*Fig. 1*). It lists some thirty-five tribes, some of which are also mentioned by Bede, whose territories can be plotted on the basis of place-names. This map reveals the existence of some very large kingdoms, amongst them those of the West Saxons, Mercians, Northumbrians and East Angles, and some very small ones, particularly around the area of the Wash, whose names are not so familiar: the Wigesta, the Wixna and the Gyrwa, for example.

One much-used metaphor to describe this situation likens it to the third round of the FA Cup: a point when many lower-division teams still remain in the competition, but are increasingly drawn against bigger and more successful clubs, who invariably knock them out of the competition. Larger teams, more often than not, can draw on greater resources and better players, a bigger fan-base, and have first pick of the most lucrative sponsorship deals, and so it seems to have been with this process of kingdom formation. The Tribal Hidage is in fact a kind of taxation document listing the relative 'value' of each listed tribe in a unit of assessment known as a 'hide'. A 'hide' was a land valuation based on the notional amount of produce needed to support an extended family for a year. It is generally thought that in Wessex a hide was roughly 48.56ha, but in less productive landscapes they might have been far larger. Matters are more complex in Kent, where the value of land was usually estimated in *sulungs* which, in the early ninth century, appear to have been the value of two hides, but by the tenth century may have been more or less equivalent with a hide.

Hides were used to calculate tax or military and related labour services, and from the Tribal Hidage assessment we can calculate the relative resources each tribe could lay claim to. They appear to have varied enormously: at the top of the list the more powerful tribes of the Mercians and West Saxons were assessed at 30,000 and 100,000 hides respectively, but near the bottom the aforementioned Hicca were valued at only 300 hides. According to this scale, Kent was the fourth wealthiest kingdom, assessed at 15,000 hides.

Aside from land and people, bigger kingdoms could also use wars to gain control of strategic resources. There was almost incessant fighting between the major players over rich estates and institutions as well as mercantile settlements. Battles recorded between the Kentish and West Saxon kings in the 680s probably led to the loss of the monasteries and estates that had been set up by Egbert I (664–73) in Surrey, as well as – following Cædwalla (*c.*659–89) of Wessex's invasion of the Isle of Wight in 686 – any remaining links between Kent and the south coast. Perhaps of even more significance to the Kentish kings, the effect of losing the powerful emporium of *Lundenwic* to the Mercians simultaneously broke its monopoly over cross-Channel trade, and severely restricted the ability to control the major trading artery inland along the Thames, drastically curtailing its sphere of economic influence. By 689/90, East Saxon kings under Mercian overlordship were active in western Kent, and King Æthelred I of Mercia (675–704) was even to be found arbitrating on the income of the religious communities of Minster-in-Thanet and Reculver.

How much these changes were precipitated by or contributed to the problems encountered by the Kentish royal house over this period is not clear. Already in 664/667, two royal cousins – Æthelberht and Æthelred – were murdered in the royal hall at Eastry, perhaps because they were plotting against Egbert I. Despite this drastic intervention, Egbert only managed to secure the throne for a short period before his own untimely death. His young sons, Eadric and Wihtred, were overlooked in the succession in favour of Egbert's brother Hlothere (674–86), thereby festering resentments that eventually saw Eadric (686–87), with the help of the South Saxons, rising against his uncle and killing him. During the confused period of warfare that followed, a West Saxon junior king Mul, brother to Cædwalla, was even briefly to occupy the throne. Only with Wihtred's reign (690/1–725) did a measure of stability return to the succession, but a precedent of external involvement in Kentish affairs had been established that would set the tone for the remainder of the early medieval period.

What could the Kentish kings do to withstand the threats from more powerful neighbours? They could certainly mobilise military resources. One good piece of evidence that kings were doing just that comes from documents of the mid-eighth century onwards, recording 'three common burdens' placed on individuals and institutions. These burdens were the military duties of bridge-building and repair, the defence of fortifications, and service in the king's army. Of these, army service is already mentioned in the laws of King Ine of Wessex in *c*.AD 694, but fortification- and bridge-work may well have been new additions to the obligations imposed by kings, first in Mercia, and from AD 792, in Kent. Archaeologically, support for this process might be seen in the construction of major border boundaries in the eighth and early ninth centuries between kingdoms such as Wat's and Offa's Dyke between Mercia and Wales, and the Wansdyke, between Mercia and Wessex. It is to this time that we should probably also date the linear earthworks of the *Faestendic* in the Cray Valley near Bexley (*Plate 11*) and another crossing the ancient routeway now fossilised as the A25 on the Surrey/Kent border near Westerham. These still-substantial bank and ditches seem to demarcate rival territories, defining the place where ownership and jurisdiction began and ended. Significantly, they are arranged to block entry into Kent, emphasising the perception of a kingdom increasingly under siege.

Another important document provides further evidence for the militarization of Kent. The Rochester Bridge burdens, documented from the 790s, record the obligation to repair and maintain the Roman bridge over the Medway. Compiled in the eleventh century, the 'Rochester bridgework list' records nine piers, the amount of wood required to span them, and the various estates on whom this burden fell, an arrangement that has been convincingly reconstructed as a horizontal wooden beam structure utilising the Roman masonry piers as supports. With a fully-operational bridge at Rochester in place, not only could Kentish kings quickly deploy troops across the Medway, they could also block the movement of ships up-river, thereby protecting the upper reaches of the Medway from naval assault.

Not all responses to the political crises of the seventh and eighth centuries were military in nature. In some cases the political status quo was maintained through diplomacy. Both Bede and the *Chronicle* record the numerous intermarriages between powerful dynasties, and it is likely that allegiances and treaties were also accompanied by the exchange of diplomatic gifts. It is by these kinds of mechanisms that Byzantine silver, foreign gold coins such as Byzantine *solidi*, Frankish *trientes* and other exotica ended up in wealthy graves such as those at Sutton Hoo, Prittlewell and Taplow. But we also hear from written sources about an agreement between King Offa of Mercia and Emperor Charlemagne of Francia for the exchange of 'black stones' (probably lava quern stones) from the Continent to England for English cloaks.

Finally, kings could shore-up support at home, and three developments of the Middle Anglo-Saxon period demonstrate these processes to good effect: the organisation of the landscape into productive units or estates; the development of urban places and mercantile centres; and an increasing concern for one's spiritual well-being, evidenced in the rapid expansion of the Christian Church.

Estate centres and the organisation of landscape

Some new written sources

In the late seventh century, a new addition to the repertoire of written sources is encountered: charters. The term charter refers to a document recording the conveyance of land or privileges by a king to a religious house, or to a lay beneficiary. About 1500 of these charters, dating from between the last quarter of the seventh century and the Norman Conquest, have survived in original form or as later copies. They provide a wealth of information about political circumstances, land ownership, and individuals named as the witnesses to the agreements documented. This latter element of charters has been used to understand the workings of royal and local courts, aspects of social structure, and some of the relationships between named kings, churchmen, laymen and women. More significantly for archaeology, charters frequently also record the boundaries of the estates in question, thereby providing a contemporary description of the parcels of Anglo-Saxon landholding. Charters record estate boundaries by describing notable features on the perimeter of the estate. The clause will generally run clockwise and tends to start and end at one corner of the estate. Many local historians have sought to correlate these boundary clauses with the modern landscape, in so doing creating a map of Anglo-Saxon landholding.

The introduction of charters in the late seventh century suggest that there was an increasing need to document the limits of ownership and the rights and privileges over landed resources. Many charters concern the Church, and it is no coincidence that they record the conveyance of rights *ius perpetuum*, for eternity. Unlike most secular land, which was required to stay within the family, and would always revert back to kin on the death of its owner, the Church needed to have its rights over land explicitly fixed. These lands were not inherited, but acquired (usually from kings), and charters provided proof of their acquisition.

'Multiple estates'

During the seventh and eighth centuries, royal and ecclesiastical estates could encompass significant tracts of land, far larger than the manorial units that are recorded in Domesday Book. These large estates were the basis of the Anglo-Saxon productive landscape, and the mechanism by which tribute was extracted. An essential feature of many estates was that they laid claim to a range of resources commonly combining arable areas of lowland with pastoral uplands. It is because of their claim to different types of resources that they are sometimes referred to as 'multiple' or 'federate' estates. At the centre of these estates existed important central places that were linked to smaller settlements; hamlets and farms differentiated according to their economic role. In some instances these linked settlements came to be fossilized in place-name or boundary evidence recorded in charters, suggesting that the estates were well-defined functional units incorporating economic and administrative roles.

One place-name element that is regarded as evidence for the 'multiple estate' is the habitative Old English element *wic*. The most common significances of the word refer to a building or collection of buildings for specialised purposes. Usually this means a dependent farm or specialised settlement, often with specialised industrial or commercial functions, such as Nantwich 'salt production site', Hardwic 'sheep-farm', Cowick, Oxwic, Woolwich, Berwick 'barley farm', Chiswick 'cheese farm'. In some cases, it seems that international maritime trade and marketing functions were the specialist purpose, as we have already encountered in the case of coastal emporia such as London and York (chapter 4). Importantly, the recognition that these sites are regarded as specialised settlements relates them to a wider economic system. This relationship is clearest with places named Westwic, Eastwic, or Norwich, which even specify the geographical position relative to an estate centre.

Estate centres were the places through which subsistence surpluses were collected and consumed. But there is evidence that the kings and elites who used these estate centres were not themselves engaged in agriculture. Most of the putative estate centres in Kent, and particularly those that may have existed from as early as the sixth century, are located on relatively poor agricultural soils (*Fig. 28*). If we analyse the location of estate centres to data from the national SoilScape (NSRI copyright) soil fertility survey, there is a clear

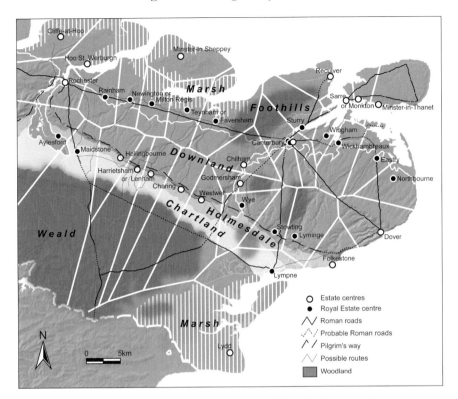

Fig. 28. A model of Anglo-Saxon estate centres in eastern Kent. By drawing schematic hinterlands around each of the centres, the range of resources (by *pays*) underpinning individual sites becomes clearer, as does their location close to the main roads around Kent

statistical tendency for sites to be located on some of the poorest soils in the county. By contrast, estate centres dating from the later seventh and eighth centuries, many of which appear to have emerged as ecclesiastical manors, are much more likely to have occupied much better-quality soil, particularly in the Holmesdale region.

A much more important criterion for the location of the earliest estate centres was the proximity to routeways. The reason for this is perhaps self-evident. As presented in the previous chapter, the earliest kings were constantly on the move. The royal entourage – if one includes the extended family, followers and the warrior retinue – may at times have numbered several hundred persons and horses. Hospitality for such a large group could only be provided at royal estate centres, in the nascent towns, or royal monasteries. Clearly, royal journeys were therefore only possible with a great deal of forward planning and careful administration, and logistically necessitated the use of adequate roads. Not coincidentally then, most estate centres appear to have been located in the optimum positions of control, occupying key nodal positions in the route network around the kingdom, but crucially also on secondary routes (the B roads) that accessed the full variety of landed resources.

From the pattern of earliest estate centres we can see the likely route of royal itineration, following the Roman roads from Maidstone to Rochester, along Watling Street to Canterbury, and around the coast to Lympne. A notable omission from this circuit is the Pilgrim's Way, a long-distance trackway presumed to have its origins in prehistory, which links together many of the later estate centres of the Holmesdale, that is to say those possibly originating in the later seventh or early eighth century. Indeed, we may have corroborating archaeological evidence that the Pilgrim's Way was not routinely used until comparatively late from the recent excavations at White Horse Stone, near Boxley in Kent. At this location two (possibly three) trackways were excavated below the Pilgrim's Way. All three trackways were of post-Roman date, however closer dating was complicated by poor artefactual evidence. Nevertheless, close to the Pilgrim's Way was a Middle to Late Anglo-Saxon crossroad burial (*c.*AD 680–970) which is likely to have been contemporary with the second hollow-way – the first lying directly on the line of the present-day routeway. This perhaps suggests that the various parallel tracks that run along the top and base of the chalk scarp only became fossilised as a significant thoroughfare on its present-day alignment during the Middle to Late Anglo-Saxon period.

One further important finding from this pattern of royal itineration is worth mentioning. If we conservatively suggest that only the Roman roads linking together the earliest estate centres were regularly used by kings during the sixth and seventh centuries, we can make a further assessment regarding the reach of direct royal control. Some 59.8 per cent of all excavated individuals are located within 2.5km of this route, and 49.2 per cent within 2.5km of the estate centres themselves. Whilst we cannot necessarily assume that where people are buried is the same as where they lived, it is nevertheless significant that nearly two-thirds of all the people we know about were potentially only an hour's walk away from having direct physical contact with their king.

If the rationale of the *royal* multiple estates was both social and economic, those that were linked to early churches were on the whole much more weighted towards agricultural exploitation. The estate centres of the Holmesdale based on ecclesiastical foundations at Hollingbourne, Lenham, Charing, or Westwell occupy much better agricultural soils than their royal counterparts. Besides fields of good arable potential, in their immediate hinterland are to be found the full spectrum of agricultural and natural resources: Wealden woodland for wood and grazing; river basin meadow pasture for winter feed, reeds and rushes; chalk downland for summer grazing. By contrast, older royal estate centres in northern Kent such as Eastry relied on access to Wealden grazing in far-away Walkhurst, Sarrenden in Benenden and Henselle, and Little Hearsell in Hawkhurst parish.

In keeping with this pattern, the Church may also have championed more intensive use of the landscape. The reclamation of the Wantsum Channel and Romney Marsh to provide for better grazing appears to have begun during this period. From Ebbsfleet in West Kent also comes the remarkable discovery of a horizontal watermill, dating from around AD 700. Evidently used to harness the tidal flow, the water may have driven a mill wheel, perhaps to grind flour, or even to pull nets and traps from the sea.

What did estate centres look like? Without better archaeological evidence it is difficult to say. Excavations at Eastry in the 1970s and more recently by *Time Team* have so far failed to identify any buildings that might be contemporary with the murders of Æthelberht and Æthelred that took place there in 664/667 (see page 95, above) (*Fig. 29*). Evidence from the cemeteries that ring the modern village of Eastry, and metal-detector finds of coins in surrounding fields, attest to the fact that Eastry was an important seventh-century centre, but the settlement itself has remained elusive. Comparison with excavated estate centres elsewhere suggest we should perhaps expect a compound of rectangular timber buildings contained within some form of earth and timber enclosure. *Time Team*'s excavations on nearby Highborough Hill seem to discount this as a likely location. A better candidate is the rectangular enclosure evident in early OS maps around the former Archibshop's manor house at Eastry Court, the village church and recreation ground, identified by Chris Arnold in 1982, although exploratory excavation there revealed nothing of relevance.

More definite archaeological evidence comes from the recent University of Reading excavations at Lyminge on the site of the Anglo-Saxon double monastery reputedly founded by Queen Æthelburga in AD 633. The excavations revealed, spreading over a distance of some 150m south of the medieval parish church and its seventh-century precursor, a planned arrangement of major and minor boundaries defining both domestic zones and areas reserved for agricultural processing. Structures included what are possibly major, 20m-long granaries, and more diminutive buildings that appear to be domestic in character. Provisional dating evidence (currently restricted to coins) suggests that the main phase of occupation is restricted to the eighth and ninth centuries.

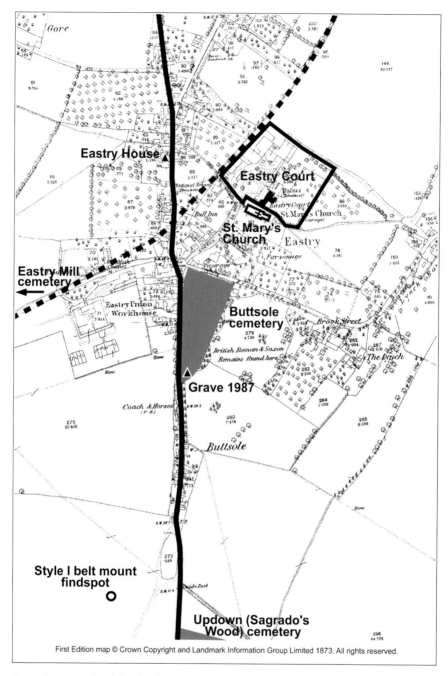

Fig. 29. A topographical sketch of Anglo-Saxon Eastry showing the location of major finds

Accompanying the occupation were over 120 rock-cut pits up to 2m deep, some of which formed dense clusters around individual structures. A proportion of the pits were used as latrines, whilst others for storage and rubbish disposal. These pits have provided a range of both artefactual and bioarchaeological data which can be used to demonstrate the scale and range of activities that took place at Lyminge (*Plate 12*). Amongst the crafts represented are fine metalworking (copper-alloy folding balance, crucibles), iron smelting and smithing, textile manufacture (loomweights, pin-beaters, needles), and leatherworking (various tools). Large quantities of quern (together with the evidence of storage) attest to the processing of grain on a scale aimed at surplus production rather than purely internal consumption.

Anglo-Saxon charters indicate that the community at Lyminge held estates on Romney Marsh (including the excavated trading/fishing establishment of *Sandtun* discussed in the previous chapter). A profusion of shellfish and fish bone finds bears strong witness to the importance of this resource in provisioning the monastic community on a daily basis. Alongside the usual domesticates consumed on Anglo-Saxon settlements, a preponderance of domesticated fowl (chicken and geese) could be taken to be expressive of a monastic lifestyle.

This evidence for intensive landscape exploitation can be contrasted with that from 'ordinary' communities, such as those that inhabited the settlement of Church Whitfield, on the Downs 5km north of Dover, in the late sixth and seventh century (continuing possibly later). Excavation of this site in 1996 revealed two timber halls constructed of earth-fast posts, approximately 4–5m wide and 11–15m long, as well as four SFBs, and a four-post structure, possibly a small granary. These types of buildings are common from other rural settlements of the Early to Middle Anglo-Saxon period, and are likely to represent a single farmstead or part of a hamlet exploiting the local downland. The halls are generally assumed to have housed a family unit, with the SFBs functioning as ancillary buildings for storage or craft activities. Here, the bioarchaeological evidence suggested that some herding of cattle, pigs and sheep was taking place, as well as some hunting, but on a much more limited domestic scale.

Hundreds and the Administrative Structure of Kent

Amendments made to Æthelberht's laws by Wihtred and Eadric in the late seventh century similarly suggest the greater concern with organising and administering the landscape. In these codes we hear for the first time of some of the procedures by which disputes were settled (see Appendices 2 and 3). In cases of homicide and enslavement, the accused must clear themselves with the help of good witnesses ('oath-keepers'), one of whom must be from his own village (Appendix 2:5). It is clear from the code that issues were tried, not on an examination of the evidence, but on the reputation of the accused and his ability to marshal sufficient support of people who were willing to vouch for him. Logistically, such oath-swearing required people to come together at designated assemblies or gatherings where the judicial process could be carried out. These places required an altar (Appendix 2:16, 3:8, 3:20, 3:21), but the context of the arrangements as they are outlined suggest that these were not necessarily in churches. Indeed, it is significant that in all of the outlined procedures justice was administered in and by the community itself, without the direct involvement of royal officials, except in cases relating to the Church or the kings' affairs themselves.

Some evidence for these administrative groupings of civil society is evident by the ninth to eleventh centuries. As recorded in Domesday Book, England was divided into shires with subdivisions termed hundreds (wapentakes in the area of Viking settlement; *Fig. 22*). Both shire and hundred possessed meeting places: normally open-air sites away from settlements, focused on barrows, stones, bridges and fords – in fewer cases in towns. (It has been suggested that the Roman amphitheatre in Canterbury may have been one such assembly place, as some of the medieval streets ignore the Roman plan but converge on the amphitheatre.) Hundreds were in general named after their meeting places; shires were named in different ways. Further sites of royal assembly, perhaps utilised only once, are also known from sources such as the *Anglo-Saxon Chronicle*, whilst sub-hundredal assembly sites are suggested by place-name evidence. Hundreds are first explicitly mentioned in a document known as the *Hundred Ordinance*, dating from King Edgar's reign (957–975), but their origins may be much older. Not all of these assembly places feature in the Domesday survey, whilst the names given to assembly sites and their associated districts indicate varied origins (pre-Roman, Roman, Anglo-Saxon, Viking), perhaps suggesting a chronological dimension to the development of administrative landscapes in England.

The hidages of the various tribal units listed in the Tribal Hidage are usually expressed in numbers which are multiples of 100, suggesting that this calculation rested on a framework that recognised hundreds (or at least hundred-like districts) as distinct administrative groups in the seventh century. We have already encountered in chapter 4 the idea that Kent may have been subdivided into smaller territorial units from an early date – the -gē districts of eastern Kent – and it is possible that some of these sub-units became fossilised in the pattern of later hundreds, as well as in a peculiar Kentish form of land division known as the 'lathe'. The districts of *Easter-gē*, *Stūr-gē* and

Lyminge are in all probability represented by the eleventh-century lathes of Eastry, Borough and Lympne, but that centred on Wester is unrecognisable due to later Anglo-Saxon administrative reorganisation. Lathes first appear in Domesday Book as large districts subdivided by smaller hundreds. Several scholars have argued that the lathes represent the primary districts of Kent, whilst the hundreds were a later attempt at administrative reorganisation, perhaps dating to the ninth or tenth century.

This perspective offers an alternative interpretation of the dynamics behind the Tribal Hidage recording, not an FA Cup style knockout competition of differently sized kingdoms, but a record of some of the sub-units that existed within larger kingdoms at the time of its compilation. A consequence of this view is that some of the smaller 'tribes' listed in the Tribal Hidage may never have had their own independent kings – political decisions being made at free assemblies if and when required. The emphasis throughout this description is on civil authority and organisation of people, not territories. It is this type of organisation of people that is enshrined in the word 'Landscape', which is a loan word from the Old Dutch *landschap*, meaning a legal territory, not the modern connotation meaning an 'area' or 'view'.

One of the conclusions to be drawn from this analysis is that it is unlikely that any kind of civil organisation included physical boundaries before the emergence of territorial administration after the seventh century. If the lathe or hundred does have some antiquity they were unlikely to have been formalised by clear boundaries before this time. However, this same evidence might be used to plot the distribution of communities existing in the seventh century, and dates the origins of the earliest boundaries at the edges of a community's territory to this time. Many of these boundaries can still be traced today: they are sometimes still evident as hedge-lines, dykes, or other physical survivals, or more commonly as the lines of parish boundaries and other administrative territories documented by the later twelfth century. Even allowing for subsequent reorganisation and change, these boundaries in part fossilise the limits of communities as they existed in the Middle Anglo-Saxon period. Indeed, unlike parts of Wessex and the West Midlands, Kent overall has fewer charters recording the break-up of older estates, often occurring in the mid-tenth century, although northwest Kent, and the coastal strip east of Canterbury, may have witnessed some reorganisation at this time.

As first recorded in maps of the eighteenth and nineteenth centuries, the hundreds of eastern Kent are particularly striking in that they are relatively small in comparison with those of other regions, in some cases only comprising two or three medieval parishes. By contrast, those of western Kent and Wealden areas appear more similar to those in many other parts of England

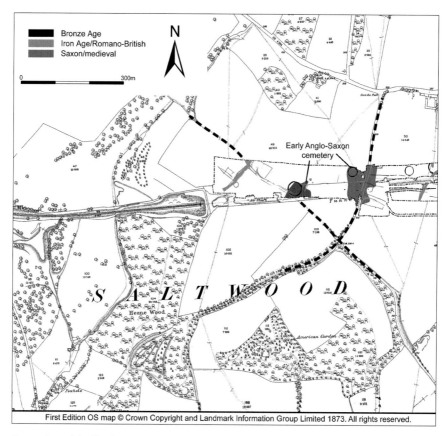

Fig. 30. A model of landscape continuity. Excavations as part of the Channel Tunnel Rail Link have demonstrated the existence of a fossilised landscape: trackways – still used when this First Edition OS map was drawn in the nineteenth century – have been revealed through archaeology to date to the Iron Age, while two groups of Anglo-Saxon burials cluster on Bronze Age barrows. These in turn became the site of a medieval open-air assembly place, remembered as 'Heane Wood', a fragment of which remains to the southwest of the excavation

and are larger and more regular in size. Possibly related to this pattern is the finding that many cemeteries in eastern Kent continued into the 'Final Phase' of furnished burial, unlike elsewhere in England where they were frequently relocated at a new site. Together these suggest that there may be considerable stability in the pattern of communities and estates in eastern Kent; the villages and hamlets of Kent – or at least the locales that they inhabit – might be seen as lying in close proximity to their seventh-century predecessors.

Evidence for just such continuity is provided by excavations which took place in advance of the Channel Tunnel Rail Link at Saltwood, 8km west of Folkestone. Here was revealed a late fifth- to eighth-century cemetery of about 219 individuals arranged in three plots, each focused on a Bronze Age barrow, to either side of an Iron Age trackway (*Fig. 30*). Significantly, the site of the cemetery was recorded as the meeting place of the local Domesday hundred, Heane (Heane Wood Barn is still located less than 250m southwest of the western cemetery), consisting of the medieval parishes of Saltwood and Postling. Very probably, therefore, this coincidence records the transition from a pagan-period folk cemetery to a hundred meeting place that continued as a centre of local administration until at least 1279.

The Kentish Church

When discussing the Church of the seventh to ninth centuries in England, it is clear that many of the functions we tend now to associate with monasteries or parish churches were not yet clearly defined. Ecclesiastical historians therefore use the generic term 'minster' to denote any kind of religious establishment with a church. Anglo-Saxon minsters were not characterised by a single type, nor were they what we understand a minster church to be today. Some may have been monastic in nature – that is to say enclosed and primarily contemplative communities cut off from the secular world. Others may have been a mix of monastic and secular roles, while some were nunneries and others bishop's seats. Pre-Viking England lacked any normative monastic rule, but individual minsters conformed to a greater or lesser degree to a liturgy and set of devotions, which may have included pastoral care to the laity. In Kent, most minsters appeared to have followed contemporary Frankish tradition, in which the minster community was made up of a mixed group of monks and nuns, presided over by a noble or royal abbess.

Minsters of the seventh to ninth centuries were bigger, more populous and more permanent than most contemporary lay settlements (it has been suggested that in some ways they should be thought of as the small towns of the period). A major religious site was not a single church, or an enclosed group of claustral buildings, but rather a series of zones surrounding the holy core like an onion. As time passed, the onion could grow further rings comprising buildings, industries and trades, which were urban in the normal sense of the word. This onion metaphor is useful, as aerial photography and map analysis has revealed that many minsters were enclosed within large precincts defined by a physical boundary. At Reculver the minster utilised the walls of the Roman Saxon shore fort as a ready-made enclosure.

Apart from the manmade site it is clear that the wider landscape took on some holy significance. Consistently, certain types of places were deliberately chosen by minster communities. Roman buildings and settlements were commonly re-used for churches and burial sites, such as at Stone-by-Faversham, perhaps to draw some link with the Christian Roman past. But most minsters also stood near water, and in Kent many are located on the marsh islands of the north coast – on Thanet and Sheppey – and this pattern continues up the Thames estuary to Bradwell, Wakering, Tilbury, and Barking. Although these minsters were not cut off from civilization, they were nevertheless exposed, in slightly marginal landscapes. In part this is likely to reflect world-renouncing ascetic ideals. Marshland isolation allowed for a life of contemplation and prayer, removed from the vices of the secular world. But island locations also meant that the holy precinct could be physically defined, in a sense as the outermost layer of the onion.

Of course the Kentish minsters were not cut off from the rest of society. The link between minsters and aristocratic women was very significant. One of the obvious secular roles for such institutions was to act as celibate havens for widowed queens, princesses and other noble ladies. These women were not for isolated hardship. Nor would they be divorced entirely from their family networks, which often stretched across the Channel to Francia. Unlike later high medieval nunneries, these were not poor, vulnerable communities of alienated women, but important political and economic central places.

They were also rich. The island-like location meant these minsters were often well placed for the exploitation of economic resources, both locally and internationally. Minsters set apart in commanding positions such as raised marshland islands could provide the focus for terrains spread with scattered farms and homestead clusters. These islands offered opportunities for economic growth – whether it was the exploitation of marshland resources or accessing lucrative trade routes between London and the Continent. There exists an important group of royal charters from the eighth century that provide good evidence that these communities were doing precisely that. They are grants for remission of tolls on ships belonging to the abbesses of Minster-in-Thanet dating from *c*.AD 730 to *c*.764 at the ports of London, Sarre and Fordwich. Another charter details a grant in favour of the church of Reculver on a ship at the port of Fordwich. It is clear from these toll-charters that the community of Minster-in-Thanet had accumulated at least three trading-ships during this period, one of which appears to have been built to order at Minster-in-Thanet itself.

The interest shown by the communities of Minster and Reculver in commercial activities seems to suggest that they were attempting to access a lucrative shipping-route from northern France through the Wantsum to London and Canterbury. Furthermore, as royal tolls were exercised on ecclesiastical trading vessels, it would appear that the Minster, Reculver and

Rochester communities were interested in selling as well as buying merchandise at the emporia of London and Fordwich. Minster's estate holdings included tracts on Romney Marsh (where sheep were already reared in large numbers during the eighth century) and on the Wantsum itself (an area of supposed Anglo-Saxon salt panning), and it is certainly also plausible that these ships were acquiring products at the continental emporia.

What did the early churches look like?

The minster precinct enclosed a church or, often, a line of churches, in addition to a range of domestic buildings. Most of these structures would have been built of wood and like contemporary secular buildings, we have very little idea about their form above ground. But the seventh century witnessed the reintroduction of masonry building to England and many of the churches were built in stone, some of which have partially survived or been revealed by excavation. The most fully understood minster precinct is that of St Augustine's monastery at Canterbury, begun after AD 598 (*Fig. 31*). By the mid-seventh century there existed here three churches, St Pancras, St Mary, and – the most important – St Peter and St Paul, which were aligned on a west–east axis. Each church was small, about 11.9m by 8.2m, and conformed to a distinct plan, recognised also amongst a number of other seventh-century minsters dubbed the 'Kentish group'.

The details that characterise the 'Kentish group' reveal strong foreign influences from Italy and Francia. Commonly they reused Roman building materials in their construction; at St Peter and St Paul the walls contained reused Roman brick and a floor of mortar and pounded brick. This may have derived from an ideological requirement, namely the belief that church buildings should proclaim something of the culture of the international Roman Church. Perhaps for the same reasons these churches drew freely on Mediterranean church designs. The plan consisted of a rectangular nave, with a wide porch at the west end and a semi-circular apse at the east end, as well as side chambers (*porticus*) to the north and south (*Fig. 32*). This design was based on churches from the Adriatic, the most complete survival being the sixth-century church of St Appolinarie in Casse, in Ravenna. Apart from St Peter and St Paul, built at the beginning of the seventh century, St Mary and St Pancras (both built *c.*AD 620), archaeologists have found similar plans at St Andrew's church at Rochester (early seventh century), St Mary, Lyminge (*c.*AD 633) and Reculver (*c.*AD 699).

In these churches, people would witness the rituals of the new religion, but for the earliest liturgy of the English Church there are few surviving texts, so we need to look at the archaeology of churches to put together an idea of how ceremonies were actually conducted. Entry to the nave was gained through the western entrance hall. The apse contained the altar, which was the focal point of Eucharistic worship. On the altar, covered by a cloth, would be candles and incense and the chalice or cup for the Eucharist wine and paten or dish for the bread. In addition, a cross, perhaps with gold filigree and garnet cloisonné, would have stood on the altar and the gospel book – such as the famous eighth-century Lindisfarne gospel – lain on it. From Reculver and Lyminge there is evidence that the apse was separated from the nave by a triple arcade of tapering cylindrical columns with ornamented bases and capitals. The columns from the Reculver arcade were only taken down in 1805, and are now in the Canterbury Cathedral crypt.

The celebration of the mass and other ceremonies required more than an altar; they required also the provision of vestments, vessels and books, and it required preparation of the sacramental elements of bread, wine and oil. These probably took place in the additional chambers (*porticus*) to the north and south of the nave. The use of *porticus* was known in the eastern Roman empire where they had ritual significance. The northern chamber was the vestry (*diaconicon*) where vestments and vessels were kept and the clergy robed themselves, the southern (*prothesis*) was where communion was prepared. The *porticus* are known in some cases also to have been used as burial chapels. At this time Roman civil law banned burial in churches so the attached chambers served as suitably honourable resting places for

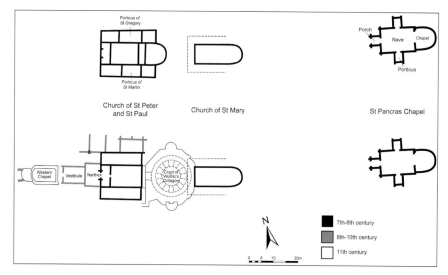

Fig. 31. Plan of the Anglo-Saxon churches at St Augustine's showing (above) the seventh- to eighth-century arrangement of churches, and (below) later Anglo-Saxon additions which refashioned the churches of St Peter and St Paul and St Mary into a single building

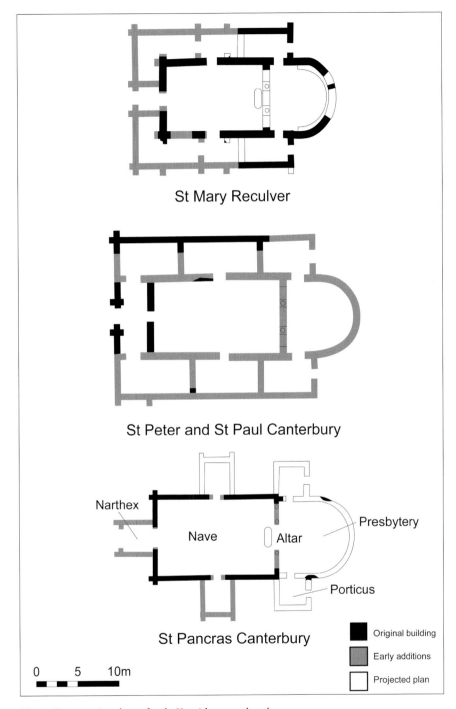

St Mary Reculver

St Peter and St Paul Canterbury

Narthex

Nave   Altar

Presbytery

Porticus

St Pancras Canterbury

0   5   10m

Original building

Early additions

Projected plan

Fig. 32. Comparative plans of early Kentish stone churches

high-ranking clergy and for the Kentish royalty. At St Peter and St Paul, five successive archbishops of Canterbury were buried in the north *porticus*, King Æthelberht and his wife in the southern slightly smaller *porticus*. This pattern of burial became popular in the seventh and eighth centuries throughout England as lesser minsters, cathedrals, and monastic sites adopted similar traditions of burial.

Towns and trade in Middle Anglo-Saxon Kent

After Canterbury became the centre of Kentish Christian life under Æthelberht, it slowly emerged as the main centre of political and economic affairs (*Fig. 33*). The building of the new cathedral in the northeastern corner of the Roman walled town, and the possible use – already discussed – of the Roman amphitheatre as the centre of the larger administrative district of the 'Borough Lathe', made Canterbury the pre-eminent centre of secular and ecclesiastical government. Allied to these functions, archaeology appears to suggest that it is over the course of the seventh century that Canterbury enjoyed an economic take-off with evidence for an increase in occupation within the walled area.

Occupation layers and a large number of timber halls and SFBs of the seventh century and later have now been found in Canterbury. These suggest that this settlement was focused in the two-thirds of the city on the eastern bank of the Stour, low-lying lands to the west having become too wet for sustained settlement. Of this eastern area, the northernmost part was almost wholly taken up by the cathedral complex, whilst to the south of this the internal arrangement of streets as we know them today also began to take shape. Castle Street, Burgate Street and Watling Street are mentioned in early medieval charters, but are not aligned on the street plan of Roman *Durovernum*. Similarly many of the excavated SFBs do not appear to honour the Roman street plan, and have in cases been found to cut through the Roman streets, suggesting that a partial re-orientation of the settlement took place during the Middle Anglo-Saxon period.

Numerous excavations have provided widespread evidence for domestic, industrial and agricultural activities taking place within the city in the seventh to eleventh centuries. Rubbish pits, courtyard metalling and boundary ditches of eighth- to tenth-century date have been found at, for example, the Mint Yard site, Longmarket, and Marlowe Car Park, suggesting that areas of dense occupation and zones of activity existed within the settlement, and that furthermore, these began to be contained within fixed building plots.

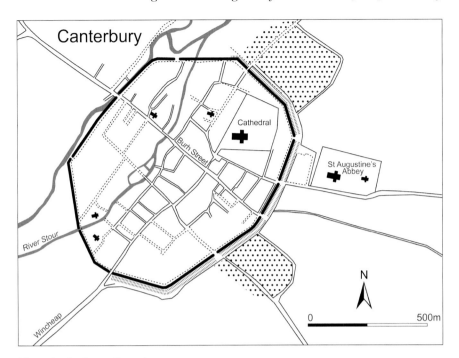

Fig. 33. Anglo-Saxon Canterbury

The Marlowe excavations demonstrated an intensification of occupation on the site in the late sixth and seventh centuries that continued into the mid-ninth century. The site also revealed some of the only known examples in Canterbury of 'post-built structures' – archetypal early medieval buildings consisting of a rectangular timber hall with a central pair of opposed doorways. The Marlowe post-built structure may have been a seventh-century workshop for iron working, which was replaced by a second structure in *c.*AD 875–900, also associated with iron working. Alongside halls, excavations have revealed a number of SFBs. Although most of the buildings had no clear function, several presented evidence of weaving activities in the locality. They were subject to periodic use, hence the evidence for discontinuities in their phasing. The weaving equipment included spindle whorls, some of which were purpose-made early Anglo-Saxon objects, others re-used Roman potsherds and another group were Roman spindle whorls, a weaving-tablet, loom weights and pin beaters, emanating from the earliest occupation layers of the SFBs.

Similar evidence for more intensive occupation at high-order settlements is evident at Dover (*Fig. 34*). So far, there is no convincing evidence for settlement at Dover before the sixth century; over the course of the seventh to tenth centuries it emerged as a major port and significant mint. The earliest Anglo-Saxon settlement appears to be concentrated within the Saxon shore fort on the west bank of the River Dour mouth. Here, excavation in the southwestern corner of the fort, in the vicinity of the medieval church of St Martin-le-Grand, has revealed a number of early medieval buildings, occupation layers and finds, dating from the late sixth to the eleventh century. Of these, SFB N3, containing a sixth-century button brooch, bead and pottery, and adjacent SFBs clearly indicated occupation in the late sixth or early seventh centuries. Roughly contemporary with these features were soil deposits found immediately outside and abutting the western Roman Fort walls. The deposits sloped down into the partly silted defensive ditch and comprised two midden-like deposits, a lower one from the late sixth to early seventh century and an upper one from the seventh to the ninth century. Whether this evidence suggests that people were tipping rubbish from within the fort, or from a so-far unidentified settlement to the west of the fort is unclear, but the evidence clearly points at the continued existence (and perhaps use) of the Roman fort walls as late as the Middle Anglo-Saxon period. However, three successive SFBs have been found cut into the

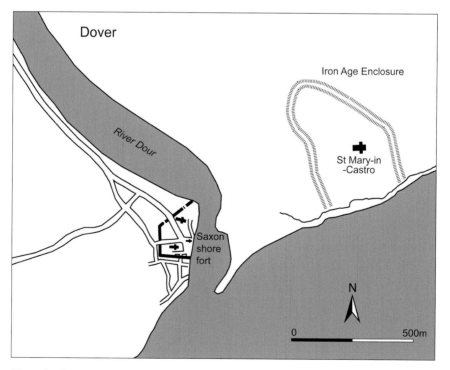

Fig. 34. Anglo-Saxon Dover

fort rampart during the seventh century, perhaps suggesting that it had a reduced defensive capability.

More significant settlement is evident in the fort area dating from the seventh to the ninth century. At this time a metalled area, a number of SFBs and a sequence of timber halls (interpreted by the excavator as a church) were constructed to the south of St Martin. These rectangular structures, the latest phase of which measured *c*.9 x 21m, were constructed in post-in-trench techniques comparable with high-status buildings identified at sites such as Yeavering (Northumberland) and Cowdrey's Down (Hampshire). The large size of these buildings may suggest that they were communal halls, possibly with annexes at either end, rather than ecclesiastical buildings associated with monastic re-settlement of Dover, believed to have occurred around AD 691. The church of St Peter (or St Martin-le-Grand) appears to be a Late Anglo-Saxon foundation, a date supported also by the presence of chalk-covered graves to the south of the church.

On this archaeological evidence, both Canterbury and Dover (as well as perhaps Rochester, although the evidence is so far lacking) appear to have been significant ninth-century settlements, apparently reviving many of the urban functions they had occupied in the Roman period. It is clear that by this time *Cantwaraburh* was regarded as the capital of a Kentish kingdom, and had begun to centralise functions (ecclesiastical, royal, economic and military) at a single site. The place-name itself suggests that the city was regarded as a tribal capital, presumably also with a defensive role. The same may also have been true of Rochester, where the Roman walls are likely to have provided a focus for local administration and defence (*Fig. 35*).

Both Canterbury and Rochester were also major mints, and the revival of monetary exchange proper provides further evidence of an economic upswing in the Middle Anglo-Saxon period. The gold coinage that briefly appeared under Æthelberht (see chapter 4) was abandoned around AD 675 in favour of a coinage of tiny silver pennies – commonly known as *sceattas*, but more correctly 'pennies' – very similar in form and weight to those found in Francia, and worth probably about a twelfth of a gold shilling (*Plate 13*). The period 675–750 saw an explosion in the scale and use of this coinage driven mainly by marketing in Kent and the lower Thames Valley. Unlike the early shillings, this money was cash proper and seems to have been used in everyday exchanges. But it is difficult to trace them to a particular mint or moneyer, as the majority are uninscribed other than with legends copied from the prototype, and it is up to numismatics to define particular series of types based on sets of specific designs. The lack of any inscription, including royal name, further complicates that situation as it raises the possibility that

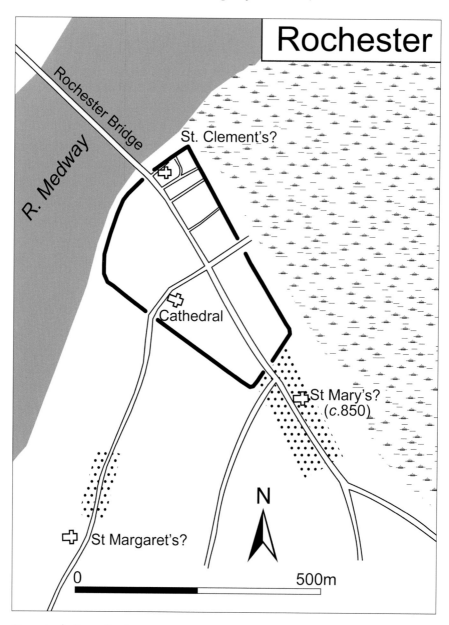

Fig. 35. Anglo-Saxon Rochester

sceattas may not have been royal issues, and that there was a degree of imitation that took place by autonomous local moneyers. By the middle decades of the eighth-century kings had, however, taken firmer control of minting. This period saw dramatic debasement and decline in the weight standard of *sceattas*, forcing the introduction of a new broader penny that was much more tightly regulated. Canterbury was one of the main mints of the new coinage, and in Offa's day had seven mints – only one fewer than London.

The development of coinage through this period parallels the evidence for international trading, described in the previous chapter. In concentrating trade and market exchange at high-order sites, and regulating the coinage used for marketing, kings of the seventh to ninth centuries appear to have tightened their grip on the economic structures of their kingdoms. The eighth-century charters detailing the remission of tolls on ships belonging to the abbesses of Minster-in-Thanet could also be seen in this light. By effectively guaranteeing free trade to Minsters' ships at the ports of London, Sarre and Fordwich, kings were offering incentives to use their settlements as centres of commerce.

The wealth generated by the economic upswing enabled amongst other things a flurry of church-building. Canterbury Cathedral is known from excavation to have had major additions, including a possible mausoleum during the seventh or eighth century, and underwent a major rebuild including the construction of a central tower in the early ninth century. To the south of the city, St Mildred appears to have been a major foundation, on or near the site of the present parish church, dating to the early eighth century and recorded as a minster in the ninth. (This church was destroyed by fire in 1246, but the present St Mildred still retains Roman tiles and quoins of Roman oolite that may have come from the original structure.)

A Failing State?

Over the course of the Middle Anglo-Saxon period, the kingdom of Kent increasingly failed in the most critical of state functions: ensuring the security of its citizenry. From the mid-seventh century onwards, cross border infiltrations became, if not a regular, then certainly a periodic threat to the individuals and communities of Kent. But in many other respects the kingdom appeared remarkably robust. Through the codification of predictable and systematized methods of adjudicating and settling disputes, kings of Kent established an enforceable body of law, including the security of property, and a set of norms that prevented the escalation of crime and its related dangers. The economy of Kent, so long dependant on Francia, became more inwardly focused, but perhaps also more stable as a result. It may also have had an effect on inequalities in society. In shifting the economy more towards landed resources and productive commodities, wealth was less likely to be polarized by access to communication networks and foreign trade. The process of dividing and allocating rights to commons and landed resources reflect this trend, as does the widening reach of the market. Finally, in the Christian Church the people of Kent were given an ideology which not only legitimised the authority of the state and its institutions, but provided direction and guidance on the changes taking place in society.

Evidence from the treatment of individuals in death suggests that society was being reconstituted from the bottom up. For the period after *c.*AD 630, the burial record for Kent charts the Final Phase of furnished inhumation. Cremation seems to have run its course, although burials from Old Westgate Farm, located only 450m northwest of the Canterbury city walls, seem to indicate the re-use of a Roman cremation cemetery for both inhumations and cremations dating probably to the first half of the seventh century. The sites that are in use in this phase include the type IV barrow cemeteries at Breach Downs, Adisham Down, Kingston Down, Chartham Down and Barfreston. The sites at Buckland, Dover, Finglesham, Polhill, Cuxton, Crundale, Broadstairs St Peter's Tip and Sibertswold also continue to varying extents. Only approximately 250 burials can be confidently placed in the period from *c.*AD 630 up to *c.*725, although those with a more imprecise dating only to the seventh century number over 2000. About fifty each of those probably dating to the last two thirds of the seventh century are of males and females, with the remainder of unidentified gender.

The furnished burial rite is noticeably in decline here, but a range of non-dress items are still present and bodies are probably still fully clothed, although the frequency of pins found on the body would indicate that shrouds may have been used. Wooden coffins are a consistent feature, as are bags, boxes, tools, and animal bone, with a considerable number of unidentifiable, small iron objects. Knives are the most frequent accompaniment. There are very few brooches, some outdated and probably kept as keepsakes. With the females, beads are still to be found, many of them plain coloured glass, but including ones of amethyst, silver and solid gold. These raw materials recur as a range of pendants and necklace components, some demonstrating fine filigree work in gold with inset garnets. Chatelaines with keys and more rarely shears are also present. An item unique to this period is the thread box, a small copper-alloy two-part canister, usually worn suspended from the waist. Their contents varied, but would probably include scraps of cloth, threads, seeds and indeterminate organic substances. Initially identified as work boxes for embroidery or repair, they are more likely to have been used as containers for items of amuletic value. For the males, the weapon sets exhibit a pattern of consolidation amongst a few individuals. Certainly single spears are found, but in smaller numbers than in previous decades. Sword burials continue, although there are only about fifteen for this period, set against over 180 known from AD 450–700. Each of these men had a shield boss, many of them also had one or more spears and there is a clear association with imported Frankish wheel-thrown pots and bottles. They are of a restricted geographical distribution, on the Downs at Breach Downs (two), Sibertswold and around the coast at Broadstairs (four), Finglesham, Ozengell, Saltwood (two) and Sarre (four).

Against the general pattern these burials appear in many respects to be old-fashioned, deliberate throwbacks to an earlier pagan age. Perhaps it is significant that they are found close to the coast, in an area where contact with foreigners was more likely – contact that may either have encouraged or provoked a form of localised posturing. Whatever their reasons, it was to be their last hurrah in a rapidly changing world.

CHAPTER 6

——— ·•• ———

THE END OF
THE KINGDOM OF KENT

The Viking Threat

It was probably just before AD 792 that Viking raiders first attacked the coast
of Kent, emerging from the sea in dragon-prowed longships. Although we
have only garbled testimony of the scale of these raids in the *Anglo-Saxon
Chronicle*, their effects on the people of Kent would be long-lasting. By
the end of the ninth century, the Kentish Church lay in ruins, the minting
of coins and international trade had all but ceased and the Kentish kings
were reduced to vassalage under a new English royal house. Not all of these
outcomes were directly attributable to the Vikings, but their activities contributed to a military and economic struggle that was ultimately to leave
the West Saxon kings in overall control, and Kent as a minor territory of
Greater Wessex.

Southeast England and Kent in particular provided an attractive target for
sea-borne Viking bands in the ninth and tenth centuries. The wealthy minsters of Kent were often located in exposed coastal positions, and these are
known to have been the victims of numerous raids during the early ninth
century. In AD 804, the nuns of Lyminge were granted refuge within the
walls of Canterbury as a result of these activities whilst, in 811, Kentish forces
were mustered to repel a Viking army on the Isle of Sheppey, presumably
with Minster in their sights. Further specific attacks are mentioned during
835 (again on Sheppey), 841 (Romney Marsh and Kent), 842 (Rochester),
851 (Canterbury and Sandwich), 853 (Thanet) and in 865, when the whole
eastern kingdom of Kent is recorded as having been ravaged (*Fig. 36*).

Raiding Kent was likely to have been a profitable exercise for most of
the period. At the beginning of the ninth century, the holdings of the great

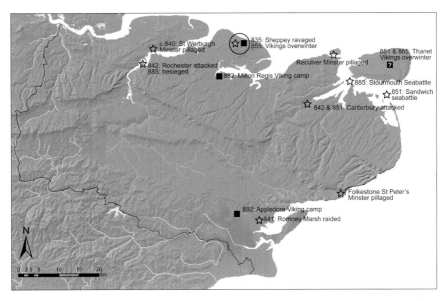

*Fig. 36.*Viking attacks on Kent in the ninth century as recorded in the *Anglo-Saxon Chronicle*

monasteries of St Augustine's and Minster-in-Thanet rivalled those of Christ Church, with those of Lyminge and Reculver not far behind. By the late ninth century these institutions were largely destroyed. There are no records at all in the ninth century of the communities of Minster-in-Sheppey and Hoo St Werburgh on the exposed Swale coast, and it is possible that members of the former had been moved to St Mildrid's in Canterbury by this time. The vulnerable location of Reculver must have meant the community was much depleted if it continued at all, and although Folkestone, Dover and Minster-in-Thanet survived some time longer, they all disappeared from records in the second half of the ninth century. Inland monasteries are unlikely to have fared much better. It is doubtful that St Augustine's outside the walls of Canterbury survived the wasting of the city in 851, and Lyminge is ominously last mentioned in 844. Even behind the walls of Canterbury the image painted by Nicholas Brooks of the Christ Church archives in the last quarter of the ninth century is one of a crisis, not only in the levels of scholarship and literacy, but of the physical community itself.

Indeed, beyond the easy-pickings of the monasteries, Canterbury itself was a lucrative target for military expeditions. In the early ninth century Canterbury was a dominant Anglo-Saxon mint and a major centre for trade, its standing in no doubt due to its proximity to neighbouring Francia. Access to this trade corridor, continuing up the Thames to Rochester and London – significant mints in their own right – was a major source of conflict between Mercian and West Saxon kings in the early ninth century, and offered an equally attractive target for opportunistic raiders. Viking attacks certainly had an effect. The debasement of Canterbury issues witnessed from *c.*AD 842 has been attributed to the interception of Continental bullion bound for Kent, and the same may have caused the temporary closure of the Canterbury (and Rochester) mints in the last quarter of the ninth century.

The value of Kent to Viking raiders lay not only in its wealth, but also its position at the head of a number of major communication routes. Inland lay Canterbury and the Pilgrim's Way – the main land-route leading along the crest of the North Downs into the heart of Wessex. But it was its location on sea-lanes that made Kent particularly strategic. Proximity to mainland Europe meant that Kent was positioned on many of the main routes between England and the Continent. Control of Kent meant control of cross-Channel sea-lanes, but its location on major maritime routes meant also that Viking forces here could move in one of several directions: inland or around the south coast into Wessex, north into either the Thames or East Anglia, or south and east into Francia. This position, coupled with the ready availability of defendable island sites along the relatively isolated Kent coastline, is likely to have influenced Viking decisions throughout the ninth century. Forces based in Kent could exploit opportunities on a number of fronts, but it also provided an exit-point when the threat of English retaliation escalated dangerously.

Some sense of the strategic value of these islands can be gained by assessing the time Viking ships took to cover distances at sea. Experiments with replica boats based on the archaeological remains of vessels, as well as the writings of contemporary seafarers, such as the Norwegian merchants Ohthere and the Anglo-Saxon Wulfstan, suggest that under ideal conditions Viking ships could maintain a speed under sail of around 5–7 knots during a day's sailing of sixteen hours. Sailing at an average of 178km per day, with the wind abeam or on a stern quarter, Viking fleets could be in Kent from Denmark in five and a half days. From a base camp on Thanet, Paris, Southampton, the Wessex heartland, and Dorestad – the major port of Frisia – would all be less than three days' journey away.

It is not surprising, therefore, to find the Viking armies establishing a more sustained presence in Kent during the ninth century than in many of the other English regions. As early as AD 811 they are known to have built fortresses on the north coast, and large armies are reputed to have over-wintered on the islands of Thanet in 851–2 and Sheppey in 854–5 – long before the more sustained campaigns of 864–878 and 891–6. Unfortunately these camps are only known from written sources; archaeology has remained silent on their whereabouts. One possibility is that they have been lost to coastal changes – up to 2km of the north and east of Thanet has been lost since the Roman period. It is certain that the island location was attractive for over-wintering, offering protection behind many square miles of marsh, bog and whirlpools.

At this stage of the conflict, the Vikings appear to have comprised small warbands exploiting opportunities for plunder and trade. Whilst occurrences of the latter are rarely described in contemporary sources, there is no reason to presume all contact with the Vikings necessarily led to violence. The term 'Viking' appears to have described all manner of opportunists (Scandinavian and Mediterranean) who were on expedition abroad, which could include marauding, but also other piratical activities, such as trading or simply thieving.

Certainly these were violent times. Although actual archaeological evidence for the Vikings is limited in Kent, there are a number of hoards known, particularly from the West Kent coast, which suggest that some individuals encountered trouble preventing them from recovering their buried treasure. One spectacular hoard, discovered in Gravesend in the autumn of 1838 and probably dating to *c.*AD 871, comprised some 540 mostly Anglo-Saxon coins, including 429 pennies of Burgred king of Mercia (852–874), together with gold and silver ornaments. It presumably represents an accumulation of valuables hidden from marauders – or the hoard of a Viking raider himself!

Unlike areas in the Danelaw, the Vikings made little impact on the place-names of Kent. There are only a few place-names with a potential Scandinavian origin, such as Cuddymill, or the Rochester street-names: Cheldergate and Broadgate. One interesting exception is a large boat-shaped earthwork which stood until the 1950s on a spit of land opposite Harty Island, overlooking the main waterways into London, called Nagden's Bump, which is a Scandinavian place-name meaning 'small pointed stone on a hill'. Given that there are so few Scandinavian place-names in Kent, it has been suggested that this singular example might point to the location of a Viking lookout or cairn, perhaps related to a Viking presence on the islands of the north coast.

How did the English kings react to these Viking threats? Initially it appears that they organised their communities to take refuge in defended places such as Roman towns and prehistoric hillforts. During the early ninth century, Canterbury first appears as *Cantwaraburh* (the stronghold of the people of Kent) in written sources, and it was there to which the nuns of Lyminge – and probably those of Minster-in-Thanet too – were evacuated in AD 804. At around the same time in the kingdom of Mercia, several important sites had new bank and ditch defences thrown up around them. But over the course of the late ninth century, under the aegis of King Alfred and his son Edward the Elder, defence against the Vikings became more elaborate and strategic. According to his biographer Asser, Alfred is said to have ordered the construction of a number of garrisoned fortifications, or burhs, from one of which, Athelney in the Somerset marshes, he began his counter-attack against the Vikings in AD 878. Following his subsequent defeat of the Viking Guthrum at Edington, a treaty was struck at Wedmore which saw the partition of England into two halves: the English south under the control of the West Saxon king; and the north – or Danelaw – under the Viking Danes. In the English half, Alfred pushed forward with his military reforms, including the expansion of his burh-building policy, and the creation of a fleet of innovatively designed long-ships aimed at challenging contemporary Viking naval power. Further evidence for these reforms is provided by an early tenth-century administrative document, known as the 'Burghal Hidage', from Edward's reign, which gives details about the ambitious nature of this scheme. The Burghal Hidage lists some thirty burhs in Wessex and the taxes (recorded as numbers of hides) assigned for their maintenance (*Fig. 37*). These strongholds, as David Hill has shown, were organised to a clear strategic principle. They were located no more than forty miles from one another and could therefore be relieved by neighbouring garrisons and supplies within two days. Many were sited to protect the entrances to navigable waterways and sheltered landing places, such as Portchester, whilst others, such as Oxford and Lewes, commanded positions astride major inland routes and waterways.

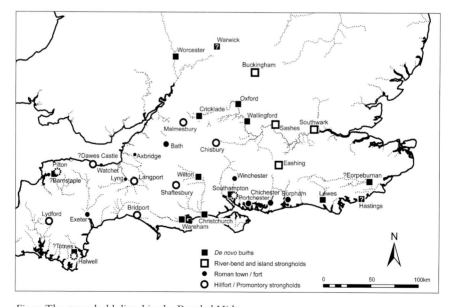

Fig. 37. The strongholds listed in the Burghal Hidage

Archaeological evidence suggests that this scheme coupled strategic aims with military expediency. In addition to new fort building, often pre-existing strongholds were incorporated into the network of defences. The protection offered by the walls of several former Roman towns took on new importance in this hostile environment and it is likely that the circuits of towns such as Exeter and Bath were refurbished at this time. At Winchester it is possible that the internal layout of the Roman city was substantially reorganised around a new, more regular street plan, with roads around the insides of the walls providing easy access to the city defences. Similar reorganisation has also been seen at Bath and Chichester. At Wareham, Wallingford and Cricklade, new burhs were raised based on a similar regular plan, comprising a central road crossing, long rectangular insulae and a series of earth and timber defences. In addition to these major works several sites appear to have been refurbished for use within the defensive system. The Roman forts of Portchester at Portsmouth and *Clausentum* beside Southampton appear to have been used as refuges, as do the Iron Age hillforts of Burpham (Sussex), Chisbury (Wiltshire), and Pilton (Devon), amongst others.

Between these major strategic sites there existed a complex network of communications and signalling positions. Although not recorded in the Burghal Hidage, these have been identified in a number of recent studies. This appears to have included networks of local forts and strongholds, beacon sites and lookouts, as well as military roads (*herepaths*), bridges and fords. Overall, the emerging picture is one of a complex arrangement of military cover representing a systematic approach to defence so comprehensive that one author has deemed it 'Fortress Wessex'.

Despite the apparent logic of this defensive cordon it is, however, striking that 'Fortress Wessex' does not protect all of those territories under West Saxon control following the Peace of Wedmore in AD 878. In English Mercia three further burhs are recorded in the Burghal Hidage, and ten fortresses are mentioned in the *Anglo-Saxon Chronicle* as having been built in the early tenth century, hinting at the expansion of the system north of the Thames particularly under Edward the Elder and the Mercian Æthelflaed. But in the southeastern extension of Wessex into East Sussex and Kent there are few recorded defences. The Burghal Hidage lists Hastings, Southwark, and the unidentified 'Eorpeburnan' (possibly Castle Toll in Newenden) as its easternmost fortifications, leaving much of the southeast coast apparently undefended.

Archaeological evidence suggests that Kent continued to rely on its older system of civil defence into the tenth century. As part of this, the towns of Canterbury and Rochester (and possibly Dover) were clearly regarded

as major military sites. The continued existence of the Roman walled circuits of these towns demonstrates significant continuity from the Roman
to Medieval periods, and it is therefore likely that these formed the main
point of defence for the events described by the *Anglo-Saxon Chronicle* and
other contemporary documents. Canterbury's late third-century fortification
comprised some 2760m (549 poles) of defences, including a town wall of
mortared coursed flint surviving to this day to a height of some 2–3m (and in
one section to 6m) and a width of *c*.2.3m. Those of Rochester are far smaller,
at 1260m (250 poles), but include also the defended bridge over the Medway,
which is known to have been in existence from AD 792 at the latest.

It is possible that these defences were refurbished during the Viking period.
Excavations at Canterbury between Burgate and Newingate in 1954 recognised that the Roman earthen defences in this corner of the city had been
levelled, probably in the ninth century, to accommodate a gravel street over-
lying the inter-mural bank. If the Roman wall was still standing at this time
this might be evidence for the creation of a new intra-mural lane providing
access to the walls. Similar intra-mural reorganisation is visible in the Church
Lane excavations of 1977 in the far north of the circuit. Here, the internal
rampart appears to have been partly destroyed in the mid- to late-Saxon
period by a number of storage pits, suggesting that at this time occupation
was encroaching quite close to the wall. Sealing these pits was a sequence of
street-metallings that cut a terrace into the ramparts, *c*.2.5m from the back
of the wall. Similarly, the internal street plan of Rochester suggests that there
may have been some replanning of the town in the tenth century to coincide
more closely with major sites in Wessex, but there is no closer dating other
than this morphological similarity. Unfortunately, without more reliable evidence, it is at present impossible to assign a closer date to all these defensive
works, though it is likely that they were constructed in response to a specific
Viking threat either in the ninth or, more probably, tenth century.

Parts of Rochester and Canterbury remained undeveloped until the
post-Conquest period. Areas close by Worthgate in the extreme south of
Canterbury appear to have existed as open spaces, as in all likelihood did
the southeastern corner of Rochester. These intra-mural open spaces are
paralleled in other major burhs such as London and Wallingford and are
likely to have provided important spaces for refugees and livestock during
periods of warfare. As a defensive strategy this seems to have been only partially successful. It seems clear from what we know of Viking activities in
the ninth century that they were allowed to roam across much of southern
England unhindered whilst local populations hid in their defended burhs.
What is not certain is whether the great slaughter inflicted on the English

at Rochester in AD 842 or Canterbury in AD 851, as recorded in the *Anglo-Saxon Chronicle*, refers to people within the towns, or undefended suburban settlements without.

Beyond these major sites there is little evidence for the kinds of civil defensive measures seen elsewhere in Greater Wessex. West Saxon kings including Alfred must have believed that the walls of Canterbury and Rochester were effective enough to defend the metropolitan Episcopal sees from Viking attacks, and indeed the events of AD 885 were testimony to this policy. In this year, the *Chronicle* tells us, a part of the Danish army based in Belgium attempted a renewed attack on England, landing in Kent and laying siege to Rochester. This appears to have been quite a significant event. The burh defences were clearly in a good state, and the Danish army was forced, for the first time, to engage in a lengthy siege, constructing – according to Alfred's biographer, Asser – a fortress 'in front of the gate' which it was forced to abandon on Alfred's arrival with a relieving force. Asser elaborates on the victory:

> …and then the pagans left their fortifications and abandoned all the horses which they had brought with them from the Frankish empire, and also left the greater number of their prisoners in the fort, for the king had come there so suddenly.

For the very first time the burghal defences successfully repelled the invader, thereby guaranteeing that the building of static fortresses would be extended throughout the rest of England in following decades.

Only one other such fort is known to have been built in Kent during this phase of the Viking Wars. The Burghal Hidage lists an enigmatic site called *Eorpeburnan* which, because of its place in the sequence of the document, is likely to have been somewhere on the Kent–Sussex border. A good contender for the site is Castle Toll at Newenden on the edge of Romney Marsh (*Fig. 38*). A survey of the site has revealed two earthwork circuits occupying the hooked end of a mile-long spur jutting into the marsh. The stratigraphically more recent circuit is almost certainly what remains of a twelfth-century motte and bailey castle. But surrounding this is a larger earthen bank and ditch, which quite possibly corresponds in length with the Burghal Hidage assessment. Importantly, Castle Toll seems also to have formed part of the estate of Beckley, which features in Alfred's will, and is the land furthest east held by the West Saxon kings. A major fortification such as this would have required not only the land it occupied, but also access to a larger estate for a supply of building timber and produce to feed the resident garrison.

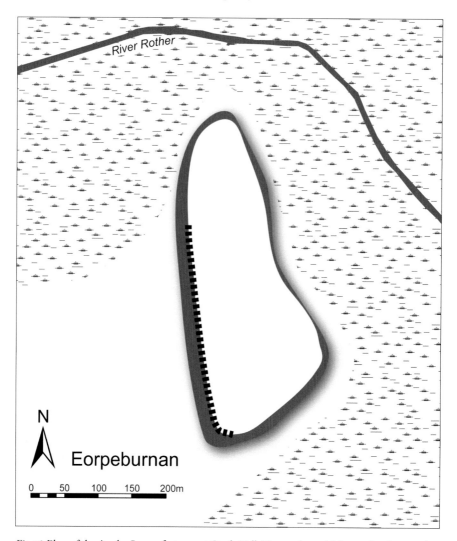

Fig. 38. Plan of the Anglo-Saxon features at Castle Toll, Newenden, which may be the remains of the stronghold called *Eorpeburnan* in the Burghal Hidage list

Castle Toll commands an important entry point into Greater Wessex. During the Viking period the River Rother had its mouth at Old Romney, and its course looped between Romney and Walland Marsh and north of the Isle of Oxney to Newenden. This placed Castle Toll at the junction of navigable water and upland, protecting access to roads through the High Weald into the heart of Kent and Sussex. Indeed, gaining access to these routes seems to have been the intention of a Viking force in AD 892. The *Anglo-Saxon Chronicle* tells us that in this year a great Viking army 'rowed their ships up the Rother as far as the Weald, four miles from the mouth of the estuary, and there they stormed a fortress. Inside that fortification there were a few peasants, and it was only half made.' The description seems to support the idea of an English fortress at Castle Toll, even if it is not the same site as the Eorpeburnan mentioned in the Burghal Hidage.

The Mercian and West Saxon kingdom of Kent

Following the West Saxon military successes of the late ninth and early tenth centuries, there followed a period of relative calm in the central decades of the tenth century. During this time Kent finally lost what remained of its independent identity, though the slide towards foreign control had begun earlier. Even before the arrival of the Vikings, Kent had begun to be subject to more powerful neighbouring forces. After the death of King Æthelberht II in 762, Kent was governed by a number of short-lived local kings who came under increasing pressure, particularly from Mercia.

The Kentish kingdom resisted Mercian advances for some time. At the Battle of Otford in AD 776 a Kentish force defeated the Mercians when much of the rest of south eastern England had fallen under their control. But such resistance was fitful. By the 780s the Mercian King Offa was ruling Kent directly and, via a number of strategic appointments, had placed Mercians in prominent positions of power. His intentions for Kent are likely to have been both strategic and economic. Many estates passed into the hands of Offa's followers at this time, including around 3200ha of land at Eastry, Ickham, Charing and Great Chart. Now we hear for the first time of provisions made for the maintenance of Rochester Bridge, facilitating the flow of traffic along the economic spine of Kent. Such ruthless exploitation of their resources did not go unchallenged by the men of Kent. Following Offa's death in 792, they reasserted their independence and ousted the Mercian archbishop of Canterbury, only to precipitate a bloody reprisal by Offa's successor, Cenwulf.

These tumultuous events underscored the course of the ninth century. Bubbling behind the turmoil of the Viking attacks, internal rivalries continued to fester and burst. A document issued in a council at *Clofesho* in AD 825 describes the situation in remarkably clear terms:

> After the death of Cenwulf, king of the Mercians, many quarrels and innumerable disputes had arisen between important men of all kinds – kings, bishops, and ministers of God's churches – concerning a multitude of secular affairs, so that in various places the churches of Christ were much despoiled in property, in lands, and in payments of all kinds.

Amidst this disorder, Kent regained a Kentish king in the person of Baldred, and the Mercian forces were dealt a humiliating defeat by King Ecgberht of Wessex at the battle of *Ellendun*, in north Wiltshire. The centre of gravity had shifted and, soon after, it was West Saxon authority that was being imposed on Kent. Following Baldred's expulsion, Kent submitted to Wessex in AD 825 and, from that time on, West Saxon kings came to regard Kent as the eastern extension of their own kingdom. Some local institutions nevertheless remained. There are grounds for thinking that western and eastern Kent continued to be regarded as separate political entities for some time longer and their subsequent divergent development over the ninth century may reflect the differing levels to which they were integrated with Wessex. Certainly the division of Kentish administration was maintained by local ealdormen. Oswulf, who held office under Cuthred (798–807), is described in a charter of AD 810 as having been king of the 'eastern province of Kent', and two separate groups of ealdormen are recorded as succeeding one another throughout the remainder of the ninth century. Under King Ecgberht, two ealdormen – Osmond and Dudda – appear at the heads of witness lists of the Kentish nobility and, as late as AD 905, the *Anglo-Saxon Chronicle* details how two ealdormen of Kent – Sigulf and Sighelm – fell at the battle of 'the Holme'.

The continued existence of a king of Kent until AD 860, and two ealdormanries through the remaining ninth century, indicates continuity in the local patterns of both administrative and military organisation. Given the location of the Burghal Hidage forts and indeed the activities of West Saxon kings in Kent, it is possible that only the weaker western kingdom of Kent was fully absorbed into the West Saxon sphere in the ninth century, with the traditionally more dominant eastern Kent continuing to be seen as separate from Wessex, despite West Saxon claims to the contrary. Alfred is certainly known to have often respected local traditions, and the absence from the Burghal Hidage of eastern Kent, London and those parts of Mercia that were known to be under the control of Wessex may reflect this. The Burghal Hidage is, however, ultimately a tax document – we may simply be seeing listed those areas that were taxed centrally by Wessex.

An alternative – and perhaps complementary – interpretation, and one which seems to be borne out in the events of the late ninth century, is that eastern Kent was under temporary Danish control. Certainly we know that the Danes were in London from 872 until its recapture by Alfred in 883 or 886. But control of London for over a decade does not make much sense without a maritime route connecting it with those detachments wreaking havoc in France and the Low Countries between 879 and 886. Danish activities during this time suggest an intention to retain control of a maritime axis with Dorestad and Frisia at one end and London at the other. Surely this could not have been realised without a sustained presence in eastern Kent – perhaps on the north coast islands of Thanet and Sheppey.

Following Alfred's victories in the campaigns of 893–7, the frontier of the Danelaw was pushed ever further north, leaving Kent to focus on rebuilding its churches and towns. In southern England, the early to middle decades of the tenth century are generally characterised by economic stagnation as the Anglo-Saxons focused on consolidation. But by the late tenth century there is an upswing in fortunes. New silver supplies from the Continent and the coinage reform of Edgar reflect a changing economic environment. It is possible that many other settlements in Kent slowly developed urban features during this time. The overriding impression gained from written and archaeological evidence is that Dover was substantially reorganised as a new town in the tenth century, possibly as a royal undertaking. Work may have started as early as the reign of Æthelstan (AD 924–39) when Dover – as *Doferi* – first appears as a named mint. By the late tenth century, during the reign of Æthelred (AD 978–1016), the programme of military construction included the building of a new beacon at St Mary-in-Castro and the refurbishment of the defences on the eastern cliffs.

St Mary-in-Castro church is a remarkable survival of this policy of national defence (*Plate 14*). This substantial church was probably connected with the refoundation of the monastic community of St Martin, which lay within the Dour-mouth settlement below, and may represent the first post-Roman settlement at the site of the later medieval castle. Intriguingly St Mary-in-Castro adjoins a Roman *pharos* (beacon), which survives to half, some 13m, of its original height. Access between the buildings was provided by a wooden gallery and an above-ground doorway at the western end of the nave, which links to an early medieval doorway piercing the *pharos* wall, suggesting the former existence of a suspended walkway. The two structures must therefore be regarded as a building complex, possibly part of a larger site defined by a pre-existing – perhaps prehistoric – earthwork. The church dimensions also suggest a defensive function: the walls are thick and are surmounted by a substantial east tower of some 21m in height. Given the presence of this second tower, it is unlikely that the *pharos* (which may well have been an even taller structure in this period) functioned as a belfry for the church, and a more convincing role as a lighthouse or beacon has been suggested.

Long-range signalling was not unusual at this time. Some two hundred years earlier, King Charlemagne is known to have ordered the repair of the Roman *pharos* at Bolougne, which continued in use as a lighthouse until 1588.

In the mid-eleventh century the German chronicler Adam of Bremen describes how the inhabitants of the island of Wollin in the Baltic (now on the border of Germany and Poland) used a 'pot of Vulcan', or Greek Fire, to guide sailors safely into harbour. It is likely that the *pharos* at Dover functioned much in the same way, providing not only a seamark for mariners at night, but also a way of signalling the approach of Viking marauders throughout the region. Charlemagne's lighthouse at Boulogne provides a further interpretation. According to plans in the sixteenth century, the Tour d'Ordre was 37.8m high which, given that it was built in twelve diminishing stages, might well have been its original height in the tenth century. This is precisely the height required to make the light intervisible with the *pharos* at Dover, some 48.2km distant. Might the reconstruction of these two towers represent the beginnings of an international defence strategy to close off the North Sea at the English Channel, thus preventing Viking hegemony around the coastline of Western Europe?

Certainly, the St Mary-in-Castro beacon seems to have been part of a wider national defensive rationale. The hilltop enclosure in which it is sited is often claimed as the location of the *burh* recorded from AD 1051, and may also be the site of Harold Godwinson's 'castle' of *c*.1064. Supporting this interpretation is the identification of a possible eleventh-century ditch, some 8m wide and 5.5m deep, forming part of the enclosure. Even without more conclusive evidence, it is highly likely that the eastern cliffs site played some part in the defence of Dover, but there is little to suggest that this position was exploited before the late tenth century. All earlier settlement evidence is focused to the west within and around the Late Roman Saxon shore fort at the mouth of the River Dour. Indeed, in this area, there is archaeological evidence for widespread destruction in the ninth and tenth centuries. A large timber hall (mistakenly interpreted as the Mid-Saxon minster of St Martin) shows evidence of having been destroyed by fire in the tenth century.

The evidence of St Mary-in-Castro indicates that Kent was being placed on a war footing in the later tenth century, and this confirms what is known from elsewhere. Wide-scale military reorganisation was taking place at this time throughout Greater Wessex, including the construction of new *burhs* (such as South Cadbury, Old Sarum, Cissbury) and the refurbishment of existing burhs like Cricklade and Wallingford. Æthelred is also known to have strengthened his naval forces in order to better defend the coast. In 1008 he ordered the kingdom to be divided into naval districts designed to construct, man and maintain the fleet. In light of the St Mary-in-Castro evidence, it is likely that this naval provision also included the creation of a formal system of coastal surveillance, with seamarks, lookouts and beacons.

As part of this enterprise, Dover must have been linked into a wider network of coastal defences. Besides Dover, Hythe, Romney and Sandwich are also recorded as having done 'ship-sokes' in the Late Anglo-Saxon period, a form of naval tax. Eastern Kent certainly was the target of renewed Viking raids at this time, and Sandwich in particular was hit in 1009, 1015, 1047 and 1048. Sandwich occupied a strategic position at the southern entrance to the Wantsum Channel, adjacent both to the Roman roads to Dover and Canterbury and the large sheltered haven of the *Meacesfleote*. Such topographical attributes secured its importance as the main naval anchorage for Anglo-Saxon fleets in the tenth and eleventh centuries.

Anglo-Saxon Sandwich is only slowly being revealed by archaeology, but it is probable that the focus of settlement migrated through the early medieval period along a peninsular jutting into the south mouth of the Wantsum Channel, an idea supported by Keith Parfitt's recent survey work here. As was discussed in chapter 4, Sandwich moved from its earlier location east of town to its present position at some point in the Late Anglo-Saxon period. There is little to date this settlement migration, but it is significant that the new site provided for more protected anchorages than the earlier location (*Fig. 26*). Also significant is the dedication of the church to St Clement, a saint who was particularly fashionable in the early eleventh century, and has often been related to Viking settlement – possibly as part of King Cnut's garrisons. The dedication might therefore provide a date for the early settlement of Sandwich at this site. The seventeenth-century antiquarian William Boys made an interesting assertion with regards to this. In a somewhat confused entry, he stated that Stonar was an older settlement to Sandwich which, after its destruction by Vikings in *c*.990, was rebuilt by Cnut. Could this be a confused tradition relating to a refoundation of Sandwich at a new location? Support for this idea comes from the earliest known residual archaeological material from within Sandwich, dated to the eleventh century.

The system was not only about coastal defence. At the same time as the construction of the St Mary-in-Castro beacon, a huge freestanding tower was built at St Augustine's Abbey outside the walls of Canterbury that may – if furnished with a bell – have been intended as a warning signal for the city. There are other examples of this sort of arrangement known also from early eleventh-century Oxford, where St Michael's Northgate tower forms part of the gateway through the rampart defences of the town.

Life on the eve of the Conquest

The emphasis on defence, and the growing sense of nationhood that accompanied it, was fuelled by economic stability. Following a period of relative stagnation in the mid-tenth century, the close of the millennium witnessed the beginnings of a period of unparalleled growth that was to last nearly three centuries.

In addition to the older urban centres of Canterbury and Rochester, there emerged in the tenth and eleventh centuries a number of new towns, all closely tied to maritime activities. Dover and Sandwich rose in prominence over the period, superseding the old port at Fordwich, and alongside them Hythe, Romney, and Seasalter represented a new chain of coastal communities profiting from sea-borne trade, fishing and piracy. Whilst these sites continued to exist under the threat of Viking attack, and this is likely to have severely disrupted overseas trade during the period, their emergence as significant centres suggests a level of defensive organisation and economic success despite the obstacles. These places ultimately provided a major stimulus to the development of Kentish towns in the later Medieval period, the Cinque Ports amongst them (*Fig. 39*).

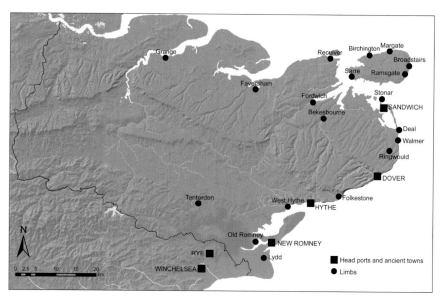

Fig. 39. The Confederation of the Cinque Ports developed out of a system of Late Anglo-Saxon coastal defence into a powerful consortium of merchant ports and 'limbs' by the twelfth century. At this time, in return for constitutional, fiscal and trading privileges, the Ports were required to provide ships and crews for the king's service – an arrangement that may already have been in existence by the mid-eleventh century

Some measure of this resurgent coastal economy is provided by the Graveney Boat found in the marshes of Hernhill in North East Kent in 1970. Carbon-dated to the end of the tenth century, the waterlogged remains of this small coastal trader contained pieces of Kentish ragstone and lava quern-stones from the Rhine Valley, as well as archaeo-botanical evidence for hops, together with twelve continental pottery shards of tenth- or eleventh-century date. Evidently the crew of the Graveney Boat had traded across the North Sea to the Rhine mouth as well as around the coast of Kent.

To some extent, kings and ecclesiastical lords deliberately fostered and encouraged the development of places in order to fuel economic growth. Seasalter first emerges as a major fish and salt market in the tenth century, which may have been founded by the king on his royal estate of the Blean, but was then given to the Archbishop of Canterbury to supply him and the monks of Christ Church with food. Similarly, the origins of Hythe are likely to be connected with royal initiatives. The main period of occupation at the fishing settlement of *Sandtun* appears to have ended *c.*850–75 (see chapter 5). Although it is not possible to attribute its decline directly to Viking incursions in Romney Marsh during the ninth century, it is likely that its vulnerability to sea-borne attacks contributed to its abandonment until the late eleventh century.

Interestingly, there seems to be some attempt made to regenerate trade in this area in the tenth century. A *Limen* coinage appears in the reign of Edgar (959–75), which may have been minted at West Hythe, Lympne or Stutfall Castle. Given the pattern of defended mints attested elsewhere during the tenth century, the latter is the most likely contender but, as yet, there is no corroborating archaeological evidence. However, by the eleventh century the main focus of settlement moved closer to the present site of Hythe, with changes in the morphology of the tidal inlet of *Limen* most probably a contributing factor. Hythe is first mentioned in a document, a possible charter of AD 1036, and was minting its own coins from 1048 to 1059, presumably replacing the mint at Lympne/Stutfall and, by the time of the Conquest, is well attested as a Late Saxon town.

Within these centres there is also evidence for economic growth. In Canterbury, excavations demonstrate moderate-to-high urban density in the Late Anglo-Saxon period. At Whitefriars, streets laid out in the eighth to ninth centuries became the focus of renewed activity following a hiatus in the tenth century. At this time, new lanes were also created and, alongside existing routes, these street frontages were colonised by a range of commercial buildings seeking to exploit the mercantile potential of the town's growing economy. Amongst these buildings we begin to see the first evidence for a distinctively urban house-type with cellar spaces. This corresponds well with existing charter evidence that details densely packed houses and streets with formal burgage plots. Domesday Book records some 451 burgesses and 187 urban properties, suggesting a lay population of at least 3000 people. To this can be added around 2000 monks and nuns, together with uncounted numbers of the poor and the unpropertied. In keeping with this figure, the Christ Church monk Osbern estimated the population of Canterbury during the Viking attack of 1011 at 8000, in other words an average density of one person per 66m².

Written sources also attest to suburban development in both Canterbury and Rochester. At *Rytherceap* outside the eastern city walls of Canterbury, a cattle market existed in the tenth century and, to the north of it, markets for salt and oats. The widened streets leading to Worthgate, Westgate and Newingate have also been argued to have been extra-mural markets. Of these, Newingate is first mentioned in a charter of the late eleventh or early twelfth century and could be a Late Anglo-Saxon insertion related to the reorganisation of the city centre. Beyond marketing, there seems also to be more industrial production taking place. At Tyler Hill, a regional ceramic industry emerged, producing pots and tiles for most of eastern Kent, whilst the iron, timber and livestock industries intensified their exploitation of the Weald.

Clear evidence of growth is provided also by the churches of Canterbury. Over the course of the tenth and eleventh centuries a number of new churches were founded to cater for the needs of the urban community. Three of the gates of Canterbury are known as parish churches from this time: Holy Cross on top of Westgate, St Mary Northgate and St Michael on Burgate. Three further gate-churches may also have Anglo-Saxon origins: St George's, St Edmund's and St Mary above Newingate, Ridingate and Worthgate respectively and five other intra- and extra-mural churches may also be of tenth- or eleventh-century date.

Canterbury Cathedral, too, is known from excavation to have undergone a major phase of construction at this time (*Fig. 40*). In the early eleventh century the cathedral saw the raising of a huge new west work, the oratory of St Mary, including a deep polygonal apse with flanking hexagonal stair-towers. Parallels for this building are found in the major churches of Ottonian Germany and represent monumental architecture of the grandest scale. The still-extant contemporary church of Hildesheim gives us some impression of how this cathedral might have looked inside. Hildesheim is entered broadwise with altars at either end so that the congregation faces Jerusalem, but the church also has the reverse orientation of Old St Peter's in Rome. Its interior is very monumental, austere, bold and simple, and much the same

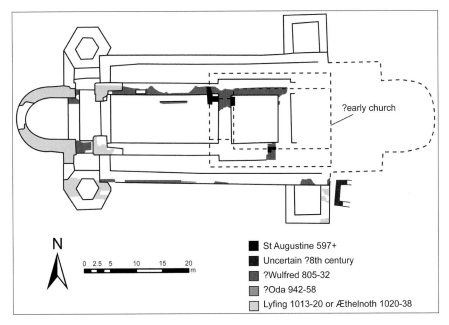

?early church

N

0 2.5 5   10   15   20
                              m

■ St Augustine 597+
■ Uncertain ?8th century
■ ?Wulfred 805-32
□ ?Oda 942-58
□ Lyfing 1013-20 or Æthelnoth 1020-38

Fig. 40. The Anglo-Saxon cathedral as revealed by the 1993 Canterbury Archaeological Trust excavations

might have been said of the interior of Canterbury which, at around 75m in length, was amongst the largest and most impressive of churches in Northern Europe at this time.

Monastic life was also revived. Following the destruction of the minster communities in the ninth century, the tenth and eleventh saw the re-emergence of monastic culture throughout Kent. Whilst some older foundations such as Lyminge and Minster-in-Sheppey appear to have survived only at a reduced status, others – such as Maidstone, Folkestone, Milton and Lympne – appear at the head of a huge group of chapels and churches in Domesday Book, and were joined by new foundations such as Lenham, Appledore, and Ruckinge.

Perhaps the clearest evidence of Kent's economic success in the Late Anglo-Saxon period is provided by the Vikings themselves. In the late tenth and early eleventh centuries, a new wave of attacks came from Scandinavia, initially aimed at extorting vast quantities of cash from the English. Between 991 and 1012 these Danegeld payments amounted to some sixty million pence, or ninety tonnes of silver. In one such raid in 1009, a Viking army fell on the citizens of Canterbury who successfully produced some £3000 (1120kg) of Danegeld to pay them off. Unfortunately for them the Vikings returned two years later to sack the city anyway.

Endings and Beginnings

The Vikings were not the only ones to recognise the wealth of the Late Anglo-Saxon state. On 28 September 1066, in a marshy, tidal inlet at Bulverhythe, between modern Hastings and Bexhill-on-Sea, Duke William landed at the head of his Norman army and went on to claim his new kingdom by force. From a Kentish perspective, it is these actions around Hastings that are particularly illuminating. Rather than marching directly to London, his first thoughts were to secure Kent and the link with Normandy. Control of this coast offered an exit-strategy should England revolt so, rather than simply accepting the surrender of Dover, he raised the town to the ground before remodelling the Castle for his own use (*Plate 15*). Kent was the bridge to Normandy and, in securing it for the French, he guaranteed that the people of Kent would look seawards and to the Continent for the remainder of the Middle Ages.

CHAPTER 7

CONCLUSIONS

The history of the kingdom and people of Kent is not unique. Throughout this book we have attempted to demonstrate that many of the factors involved in the development of Kent over the period AD 400–1066 – social, political and economic – held true also in other parts of the early medieval world. Whilst the routes these kingdoms took may often have their own distinctive trajectories and narratives, the options available to individual communities and their leaders came from a fairly narrow range of choices. Military power, the control of valuable objects, personal bonds of loyalty, and the ability to maintain access to key resources helped to define the early medieval ruler; for humble communities, the way in which they made a living in such uncertain times was the main preoccupation.

The foregoing analysis does not claim to take more than a broad view of the subject. Nevertheless, important points can be made about the development of Kent at this time. It is clear that early medieval Kentish society and economy contained elements of both continuity and transformation. Although this book has focussed deliberately on the events that took place after the ending of the Roman occupation in England, the legacy of Rome looms large in many of these chapters. The structures, landscapes and economies of the earliest Anglo-Saxon communities were – at least in part – defined by the Roman legacy. Roman roads, cities, forts and *villae*, helped to structure settlement patterns, even if this was often in subtle and understated ways. There are too many instances of discontinuity in the use and function of Roman settlement for us to deny a significant political and institutional break from the Roman past, but nevertheless we have cited examples of how Roman roads determined the routes of royal itineration, how derelict Roman amphitheatres became places of public assembly, and how Roman city walls and forts became the strongholds of civil defence.

The legacy of Rome can also be recognised in political and religious history. In many ways, Æthelberht and those like him modelled themselves on the Roman archetype as the 'Heirs of Rome', adopting the legal language (if not traditions), the intellectual stance, ideology and material culture of Roman emperors as understood at a temporal distance in the sixth and seventh centuries. Yet more convincing continuity is demonstrated by the Church itself, which despite a hiatus of nearly two hundred years, reaffirmed its place in Kentish society and its landscape to such an extent that Canterbury has ever since been synonymous with English religious life.

It is equally clear that Francia was an ever-present feature in Kentish development, both as an active political and economic force in the North Sea world of which Kent was a part, but also as the ideological successor of the Roman Empire. Events and policies in Francia were fundamentally important throughout: it was the major trading partner during Kent's rise as the premier English entrepôt in the sixth and seventh centuries; the Christian mission arrived in AD 597 from Francia and under Frankish protection, and served in time to bind England to the broader Christian Church. Individual events in Francia could also prove significant, such as in AD 892, when the Viking force landed in Kent primarily because they had been successfully repulsed by Odo, King of West Francia, or in 1066, when the Norman invasion took place. The purpose of this book is to highlight the development of a region and a people, but it is abundantly clear, given these many cross-Channel exchanges, that a more internationalist history could and should be written for us to achieve a fuller understanding of the complexities of this era.

The themes that emerge in this story have been primarily of social and economic history: what people did, how they were buried, a little of what they thought and how they lived from day to day, using the evidence of their remaining material culture. We have not attempted to provide a narrative of events except to outline the barest of political histories. In part this reflects the nature of the evidence. The dearth and unreliability of written sources for much of the period is counterpointed by an abundance of archaeological material, although this in itself is also often partial and incomplete. To address this imbalance we have endeavoured to adopt an avowedly multi-disciplinary approach, using archaeological and written sources, toponymy whenever appropriate, and drawing on debates and ideas current in historical, archaeological and anthropological literature. For those interested in reading more about these ideas and about the sources themselves, guidance is provided to the literature in the Further Reading section of this book. The history of the kingdom and people of Kent is not unique within what we know of early Medieval Europe, yet Kent is a special place precisely because of its links to the wider world.

APPENDIX 1

THE LAW CODES OF ÆTHELBERHT

[Theft of] God's property and the Church's shall be compensated twelve fold; a bishop's property eleven fold; a priest's property nine fold; a deacon's property six fold; a clerk's property three fold. Breach of the peace shall be compensated doubly when it affects a church or a meeting place.

If the king calls his lieges to him, and anyone molests them there, he shall pay double compensation, and 50 shillings to the king.

If the king is feasting at anyone's house, and any sort of offence is committed there, twofold compensation shall be paid.

If a freeman robs the king, he shall pay back a nine fold amount.

If one man slays another on the king's premises, he shall pay 50 shillings compensation

If a man slays a free man, he shall pay 50 shillings to the king for infraction of seignorial rights.

If [he] slays a smith in the king's service, or a messenger belonging to the king, he shall pay an ordinary *wergeld*.

The king's *mundbyrd* shall be 50 shillings.

If a freeman robs a freeman, he shall pay a three fold compensation, and the king shall take the fine, or all [the man's] goods.

If a man lies with a maiden belonging to the king, he shall pay 50 shillings compensation.

If she is a grinding slave, he shall pay 25 shillings compensation. [If she is of the] third [class], [he shall pay] 12 shillings compensation.

20 shillings shall be paid for killing a *fedesl* belonging to the king.

If one man slays another on the premises of a nobleman, he shall pay 12 shillings compensation.

If a man lies with a nobleman's serving maid, he shall pay 112 shillings compensation.

A commoner's *mundbyrd* shall be 6 shillings.

If a man lies with a commoner's serving maid he shall pay 6 shillings compensation; [if he lies] with a slave of the second class, [he shall pay] 50 *sceattas* [compensation]; if with one of the third class, 30 *sceattas*.

If a man is the first to make [forcible] entry into another man's premises, he shall pay 6 shillings compensation. He who comes next shall pay 3 shillings compensation, and afterwards each shall pay a shilling.

If one man supplies another with weapons when a quarrel is taking place, no injury however being inflicted, he [the lender] shall pay 6 shillings compensation.

If highway robbery is perpetrated [with the aid of those weapons], [the lender] shall pay 6 shillings compensation.

If the man is slain, [the lender of the weapons] shall pay 20 shillings compensation.

If one man slays another, the ordinary *wergeld* to be paid as compensation shall be 100 shillings.

If one man slays another, he shall pay 20 shillings before the grave is closed, and the whole of the *wergeld* within 40 days.

If a homicide departs from the country, his relatives shall pay half the *wergeld*.

If a man lays bonds on a freeman, he shall pay 20 shillings compensation.

If a man slays the dependant of a commoner, he shall pay [the commoner] 6 shillings compensation.

If he slays a *læt* of the best class, he shall pay 80 shillings; if he slays one of the second class, he shall pay 60 shillings; [for slaying one of] the third class, he shall pay 40 shillings.

If a freeman breaks the fence round [another man's] enclosure, he shall pay 6 shillings compensation.

If any property be seized therein, the man shall pay a three fold compensation.

If a freeman makes his way into a fenced enclosure, he shall pay 4 shillings compensation.

If one man slays another, he shall pay the *wergeld* with his own money and property (i.e. livestock or other goods) which whatever its nature must be free from blemish [or damage].

If [one] freeman lies with the wife of [another] freeman, he shall pay [the husband] his [or her] *wergeld*, and procure a second wife with his own money, and bring her to the other man's home.

If anyone damages the enclosure of a dwelling, he shall pay according to its value.

For seizing a man by the hair, 50 *sceattas* shall be paid as compensation.

If a bone is laid bare, 3 shillings shall be paid as compensation.

If a bone is damaged, 4 shillings shall be paid as compensation.

If the outer covering of the skull is broken, 10 shillings shall be paid as compensation.

If both are broke, 20 shillings shall be paid as compensation.

If the shoulder is disabled, 30 shillings shall be paid as compensation.

If the hearing of either ear is destroyed, 25 shillings shall be paid as compensation.

If an ear is struck off, 12 shillings shall be paid as compensation.

If an ear is pierced, 3 shillings shall be paid as compensation.

If an ear is lacerated, 6 shillings shall be paid as compensation.

If an eye is knocked out, 50 shillings shall be paid as compensation.

If the mouth or an eye is disfigured, 12 shillings shall be paid as compensation.

If the nose is pierced, 9 shillings shall be paid as compensation.

If it one cheek, 3 shillings shall be paid as compensation.

If both are pierced, 6 shillings shall be paid as compensation

If the nose is lacerated otherwise [than by piercing], 6 shillings shall be paid as compensation, for each laceration.

If it is pierced, 6 shillings shall be paid as compensation.

He who smashes a chin bone, shall pay for it with 20 shillings.

For each of the 4 front teeth, 6 shillings [shall be paid as compensation]; for each of the teeth which stand next to these, 4 shillings [shall be paid as compensation]; then for each tooth which stands next to them, 3 shillings [shall be paid as compensation]; and beyond that 1 shilling [shall be paid as compensation] for each tooth.

If the power of speech is injured, 12 shillings [shall be paid as compensation].

If a collar bone is injured, 6 shillings shall be paid as compensation.

He who pierces an arm shall pay 6 shillings as compensation.

If an arm is broken, 6 shillings shall be paid as compensation.

If a thumb is struck off, 20 shillings [shall be paid as compensation].

If a thumb nail is knocked off, 3 shillings shall be paid as compensation

If a man strikes off a forefinger, he shall pay 9 shillings compensation.

If a man strikes off a middle finger, he shall pay 4 shillings compensation

If a man strikes off a 'ring finger', he shall pay 6 shillings compensation

If a man strikes off a little finger, he shall pay 11 shillings compensation.

For the nails of each [of the above mentioned fingers], 1 shilling [shall be paid as compensation].

For the slightest disfigurement, 3 shillings, and for a greater 6 shillings [shall be paid as compensation].

If one man strikes another on the nose with his fist, 3 shillings [shall be paid as compensation].

If it leaves a bruise 1 shilling [shall be paid as compensation].

If it leaves a black bruise [showing] outside the clothes, 30 *sceattas* shall be paid as compensation.

If it [the bruise] is under the clothes, 20 *sceattas* shall be paid as compensation for each [bruise]

If the belly is wounded, 12 shillings shall be paid as compensation.

If it be pierced, 20 shillings shall be paid as compensation.

If a man receives medical treatment, 30 shillings shall be paid as compensation.

If a man is severely wounded, 30 shillings shall be paid as compensation.

If anyone destroys the generative organ, he shall pay for it with three times the *wergeld*.

If he pierces it right through, he shall pay 6 shillings compensation.

If he pierces it partially, he shall pay 6 shillings compensation.

If a thigh is broken, 12 shillings shall be paid as compensation.

If he becomes lame, the settlement of the matter may be left to friends.

If a rib is broken, 3 shillings shall be paid as compensation.

If a thigh is pierced right through, 6 shillings compensation shall be paid for each stab [of this kind].

For a stab over an inch [deep], 1 shilling; for a stab between 2 and 3 inches [deep], 2 shillings; for a stab over 3 inches [deep], 3 shillings shall be paid as compensation.

If a sinew is wounded, 3 shillings shall be paid as compensation.

If a foot is struck off, 50 shillings shall be paid for it.

If the big toe is struck off, 10 shillings shall be paid for it.

For each of the other toes, [a sum] equal to half that laid down for the corresponding fingers shall be paid.

If the nail of the big toe is knocked off, 30 *sceattas* shall be paid as compensation.

10 *sceattas* shall be paid as compensation for the loss of each of the other toenails.

If a freeborn woman, with long hair, misconducts herself, she shall pay 30 shillings as compensation.

Compensation [for injury] to be paid to an unmarried woman, shall be on the same scale as that paid to a freeman.

The compensation to be paid for the violation of the *mund* of a widow of the best class [that is, of a widow] of the nobility, shall be 50 shillings.

For violation of the *mund* of a widow of the second class, 20 shillings; of the third class, 12 shillings; of the fourth class, 6 shillings.

If a man takes a widow who does not [of right] belong to him, double the value of the *mund* shall be paid.

If a man buys a maiden, the bargain shall stand if there is no dishonesty.

If however there is dishonesty, she shall be taken back to her home, and the money shall be returned to him.

If she bears a living child, she shall have half the goods left by her husband, if he dies first.

If she wishes to depart with her children, she shall have half the goods.

If the husband wishes to keep [the children], she shall have a share of the goods equal to a child's.

If she does not bear a child, [her] father's relatives shall have her goods, and the 'morning gift'.

If a man forcibly carries off a maiden, [he shall pay] 50 shillings to her owner, and afterwards buy from the owner his consent.

If she is betrothed, at a price, to another man, 20 shillings shall be paid as compensation.

If she is brought back, 35 shillings shall be paid, and 15 shillings to the king.

If a man lies with the woman of a servant, during the lifetime of the husband, he shall pay a twofold compensation.

If one servant slays another, who has committed no offence, he shall pay his full value.

If the eye and foot of a servant are destroyed [by blows], his full value shall be paid.

If a man lays bonds on another man's servant, he shall pay 6 shillings compensation.

The sum to be paid for robbing a slave on the highway shall be 3 shillings.

If a slave steals, he shall pay twice the value [of the stolen goods] as compensation.

THE LAW CODES OF HLOTHHERE AND EADRIC

If a man's servant slays a nobleman, whose *wergeld* is 300 shillings, his owner shall surrender the homicide and pay the value of three men in addition.

If the homicide escapes, he shall add thereto the value of a fourth man and prove by good witnesses that he has not been able to lay hands on the homicide.

If a man's servant slays a freeman whose *wergeld* is 100 shillings, his owner shall surrender the homicide and [pay] the value of another man in addition.

If the homicide escapes, [his owner] shall pay for him with two *wergelds* and prove by good witnesses that he has not been able to lay hands on the homicide.

If a freeman steals a man, and if he [who has been stolen] returns as an informer, he shall accuse him to his face; and he [the thief] shall clear himself if he can. And every man involved in such a charge shall have a number of free witnesses, and one [at least] of his witnesses from the village to which he himself belongs. If he cannot do this, he must pay to the best of his ability.

If a man dies leaving a wife and child, it is right, that the child shall accompany the mother; and one of his father's relatives who is willing to act, shall be given him as his guardian to take care of his property, until he is ten years old.

If one man steals property from another, and the owner afterwards reclaims it, he [who is in possession] shall bring it to the king's residence, if he can, and produce the man who sold it him. If he cannot do that, he shall surrender it, and the owner shall take possession [of it].

If one man brings a charge against another, and if he meets the man [whom he accused], at an assembly or meeting, the latter shall always provide the former with a surety, and render him such satisfaction as the judges of Kent shall prescribe for them.

If, however, he refuses to provide a surety, he shall pay 12 shillings to the king, and the suit shall be considered as open as it was before.

If one man charges another, after the other has provided him with a surety, then three days later they shall attempt to find an arbitrator, unless the accuser prefers a long delay. Within a week after the suit has been decided by arbitration, the accused shall render justice to the other and satisfy him with money, or an oath, whichever he [the accused] prefers. If, however, he is not willing to do this, then he shall pay 100 shillings, without [giving] an oath, on the day after the arbitration.

If one man calls another a perjurer in a third man's house, or accosts him abusively with insulting words, he shall pay one shilling to him who owns the house, 6 shillings to him he has accosted, and 12 shillings to the king.

If, where men are drinking, one man takes away the stoup of another, who has committed no offence, he shall pay, in accordance with established custom, a shilling to him who owns the house, 6 shillings to him whose stoup has been taken away, and 12 shillings to the king.

If, where men are drinking, a man draws his weapon, but no harm is done there, he shall pay a shilling to him who owns the house, and 12 shillings to the king.

[But] if the house is stained with blood, the owner shall have his *mundbyrd* paid to him, and fifty shillings shall be paid to the king.

If a man entertains a stranger (a trader or anyone else who comes over the border) for three days in his own home, and then supplies him with food from his own store, and [if] he [the stranger] then does harm to anyone, the man shall bring the other to justice, or make amends on his behalf.

If a man of Kent buys property in London, he shall have two or three trustworthy men, or the reeve of the king's estate, as witness.

If afterwards it is claimed from the man in Kent, he shall summon as witness, to the king's residence in London, the man who sold it to him, if he knows him and can produce him as warrant for the transaction.

If he cannot do so, he shall declare on the altar, with one of his witnesses or with the reeve of the king's estate, that he bought the goods openly in London, and with goods known to be his, and the value [of the property] shall be returned to him.

If, however, he cannot prove that by lawful declaration, he shall give it up, and the owner shall take possession of it.

THE LAW CODES
OF WIHTRED

These are the decrees of Wihtred, King of Kent.

During the sovereignty of Wihtred, the most gracious king of Kent, in the fifth year of his reign, the ninth Indiction, the sixth day of Rugern, in a place which is called Barham, there was assembled a deliberative council of the notables. There were present there Berhtwald, the chief bishop of Britain, and the above-mentioned king; the bishop of Rochester, who was called Gefmund; and every order of the Church of the province expressed itself in unanimity with the loyal laity [assembled there].

There the notables, with the consent of all, drew up these decrees, and added them to the legal usages of the people of Kent, as is hereafter stated and declared:

The Church shall enjoy immunity from taxation.

The king shall be prayed for, and they shall honour him freely without compulsion.

The *mundbyrd* of the church shall be 50 shillings like the king's.

Men living in illicit unions shall turn to a righteous life repenting of their sins, or they shall be excluded from the communion of the Church.

Foreigners, if they will not regularise their unions, shall depart from the land with their possessions and with their sins.

Men of our own country also shall be excluded from the communion of the Church, without being subject to the forfeiture of their goods.

If after this meeting, a nobleman presumes to enter into an illicit union, despite the command of the king and the bishop, and the written law, he shall pay 100 shillings compensation to his lord, in accordance with established custom.

If a commoner does so, he shall pay 50 shillings compensation; and [in] either [case the offender] shall desist from the union, with repentance.

If a priest consents to an illicit union, or if he neglects the baptism of a sick man, or is too drunk to discharge his duty, he shall abstain from his ministrations, pending a decision from the bishop.

If a tonsured man, [who is] not under ecclesiastical discipline, wanders about looking for hospitality, once [only] shall it be granted to him, and unless he has permission, he shall not be entertained further.

If anyone grants one of his men freedom on the altar, his freedom shall be publicly recognised; [but] the emancipator shall have his heritage and his *wergeld*, and the guardianship of his household, wherever he [the freed man] may be, [even if it be] beyond the border.

If a servant, contrary to his lord's command, does servile work between sunset on Saturday evening and sunset on Sunday evening, he shall pay 80 *sceattas* to his lord.

If a servant makes a journey of his own [on horseback] on that day, he shall pay 6 shillings compensation to his lord or undergo the lash.

If a freeman works during the forbidden time, he shall forfeit his *healsfang*, and the man who informs against him shall pay half the fine, and [the profits arising from] the labour.

If a husband, without his wife's knowledge, makes offerings to devils, he shall forfeit all his goods or his *healsfang*. If both of them make offerings to devils they shall forfeit their *healsfangs* or all their goods.

If a slave makes offerings to devils, he shall pay 6 shillings compensation or undergo the lash.

If a man gives meat to his household during a fast, he shall redeem [each of them], both bond and free, by payment of his [own] *healsfang*.

If a slave east of his own free will, he shall pay 6 shillings compensation or undergo the lash.

A bishop's or a king's word, [even] though unsupported by an oath, shall be incontrovertible.

The head of a monastery shall clear himself by the formula used by a priest.

A priest shall clear himself by his own asseveration, [standing] in his holy garments before the altar and declaring as follows 'Veritatem dico in Christo, non mentior'. A deacon shall clear himself in a similar way.

A clerk shall clear himself with [the support of] three of his own class, he alone [having] his hand on the altar. The others shall attend for the purpose of validating the oath.

A stranger shall clear himself by his own oath, at the altar. A king's thegn shall clear himself in the same way.

A commoner shall clear himself at the altar, with three of his own class; and the oath of all these [collectively] shall be incontrovertible.

The Church has further prerogatives with regard to expurgation, [which are] as follows:

If a servant of a bishop or of the king is accused, he shall clear himself by the hand of the reeve. The reeve shall either exculpate him or deliver him up to be scourged.

If anyone brings an accusation against a bond servant of a company in presence of the company, his lord shall clear him by his oath if he [the lord] is a communicant. If he is not a communicant he shall get a second good witness [to support him] in the oath, or pay [the fine] or deliver him up to be scourged.

If a layman's servant accuse the servant of an ecclesiastic, or if an ecclesiastic's servant accuse the servant of a layman, his lord shall clear it by his own oath.

If anyone slays a man in an act of thieving, no *wergeld* shall be paid for him.

If anyone catches a freeman in the act of stealing, the king shall decide which of the following three courses shall be adopted – whether he shall be put to death, or sold beyond the sea, or held to ransom for his *wergeld*.

He who catches and secures him, shall have half his value. If he is put to death, 70 shillings shall be paid to him.

If a slave steals, and is released, 70 shilligs [shall be paid] – whichever the king wishes. If he is put to death, half his value shall be paid to the man who has him in his power.

If a man from afar, or a stranger, quits the road, and neither shouts, nor blows a horn, he shall be assumed to be a thief, [and as such] may be either slain or put to ransom.

APPENDIX 4

THE KENTISH KINGS
AND RULERS

Early period to AD 616

Hengest; Œric (Oisc); Octa; Eormenric; Æthelberht I

AD 616–664

Eadbald; Earconberht

AD 664–725

Egbert I; Hlothhere;(Swæfheard of the East Saxons, sub-king of West Kent); Eadric; Oswine; Wihtred

AD 725–762

Eadbehrt I; Æthelberht II; Alric; Eardwulf (earlier sub-king of West Kent)

AD 765–825

Egbert II; Ealhmund; Eadbehrt II (Praen); Egbert, son of Ealhmund; Cuthred of Mercia; Baldred

AD 825–860

Æthwulf of Wessex; Æthelstan

Post AD 860

Kent loses its status as a separate kingdom and is absorbed into Wessex

FURTHER READING

Books and articles about Anglo-Saxon and Viking Age Kent

Brookes, S. 2007. *Economics and social change in Anglo-Saxon Kent AD 400–900. Landscapes, communities and exchange*. Oxford: BAR British Series 431

Brooks, N. 1984. *The Early History of the Church of Canterbury*. Leicester: Leicester University Press

Brooks, N. 1989. 'The creation and early structure of the kingdom of Kent'. In Bassett, S. (ed.). *The origins of Anglo-Saxon kingdoms*. 55–74. Leicester: Leicester University Press

Clarke, H., Pearson, S., Mate, M. and Parfitt, K. 2010. *Sandwich: The 'Completest Medieval Town in England'. A Study of the Town and Port from its Origins to 1600*. Oxford: Oxbow

Draper, G. and Meddens, F. 2009. *The Sea and the Marsh: The Medieval Cinque Port of New Romney revealed through archaeological excavation and historical research*. Pre-Construct Archaeology Monologue

Everitt, A. 1986. *Continuity and Colonization: the evolution of Kentish Settlement*. Leicester: Leicester University Press

Gameson, R. (ed.) 1999. *St Augustine and the conversion of England*. Thrupp: Sutton Publishing

Hasted, E. 1778–1799. *The history and topographical survey of the county of Kent: containing the antient and present state of it, civil and ecclesiastical*. Canterbury

Hawkes, S.C. 1982. 'Anglo-Saxon Kent *c.*425–725'. In Leach, P.E. (ed.). *Archaeology in Kent to AD 1500*. 64–78. CBA Research Report 48. London

Hawkes, S.C. 1989. 'The South-east after the Romans: the Saxon settlement'. In Maxfield, V. A. (ed.). *The Saxon Shore: a handbook*, 78–95, *Exeter Studies in History 25*. Exeter

Kelly, S.E. (ed.) 1995. *Charters of the St Augustine's Abbey, Canterbury, and Minster-in-Thanet*. Anglo-Saxon Charters 4, Oxford: Oxford University Press

Kirby, D.P. 1991. 'Early Kent' in The Earliest English Kings. London: Unwin Hyman, 30–47

Lyle, M. 2002. *Canterbury: 2000 Years of History*. Stroud: The History Press

Malcolm, G., Bowsher, D. and Cowie, R. 2003. *Middle Saxon London: excavations at the Royal Opera House 1989-99*. London: MOLAS

Ramsay, N., Sparks, M. and Tatton-Brown, T., (eds) 1992. *St Dunstan: his life, times and cult*. Woodbridge: Boydell

Richardson, A. 2005. *The Anglo-Saxon cemeteries of Kent*. BAR British Series 391. Oxford

Tatton-Brown, T. 1984. 'The Towns of Kent'. In Haslam, J. (ed.) *Anglo-Saxon Towns in*

Southern England. Chichester: Camelot Press, 1–36; also 1988. 'The Anglo-Saxon Towns of Kent'. In Hooke, D. *Anglo-Saxon Settlements*. Oxford: Blackwell, 213–232

Tatton-Brown, T. 1988. 'The Churches of Canterbury Diocese in the 11th Century'. In Blair, J. (ed.) *Minster and Parish Churches: The Local Church in Transition, 950–1200*. Oxford: Oxford University Committee for Archaeology Monograph 17, 105–118

Welch, M. 2007. 'Anglo-Saxon Kent to AD 800'. In Williams, J. (ed.).
    The Archaeology of Kent to AD *800*. 187–248. Woodbridge: Boydell Press

Witney, K.P. 1982. *The Kingdom of Kent*. Chichester: Philimore

Roman Kent

Blagg, T. 1982. 'Roman Kent'. In Leach, P. (ed.). *Archaeology in Kent to* AD *1500*. 51–60. CBA Research Report 48. London

Cotterill, J. 1993. 'Saxon raiding and the role of the late Roman coastal forts of Britain', *Britannia* 24, 227–39.

Cunliffe, B. 1980. 'Excavations at the Roman fort at Lympne', *Britannia* 11, 227–88

Detsicas, A. 1983. *The Cantiaci*. Gloucester: Alan Sutton

Millet, M. 2007. Roman Kent. In Williams, J. (ed.). *The Archaeology of Kent to* AD *800*. 135–84. Woodbridge: Boydell Press

Reports from excavations in Kent cited in the text

Bennett, P. 1988. 'Archaeology and the Channel Tunnel'. *Archaeologia Cantiana* 106, 1–24

Blockley, K., Blockley, M., Blockley, P., Frere, S.S. and Stow, S. 1995. *Excavations in the Marlowe Car Park and Surrounding Areas*. Canterbury: The Archaeology of Canterbury monograph series 5

Blockley, K., Sparks, M. and Tatton-Brown, T. 1997. *Canterbury Cathedral Nave: Archaeology, History and Architecture*. Canterbury: The Archaeology of Canterbury (New Series) 1

Clark, P., Rady, J. and Sparey-Green, C. 2009 'Wainscott Northern By-pass Archaeological Investigations' 1992–1997. Canterbury Archaeological Trust Occasional Paper No. 5

Davidson, H. and Webster, L.1967. 'The Anglo-Saxon burial at Coombe (Woodnesborough), Kent', *Medieval Archaeology* 11, 1–41

Evison, V. 1987. 'Dover: the Buckland Anglo-Saxon cemetery'. Historic Buildings and Monuments Commission for England Archaeological Report 3, London

Faussett, Revd B. (Roach Smith, C. ed.). 1856. *Inventorium Sepulchrale: an account of some antiquities dug up at Gilton, Kingston, Sibertswold, Barfriston, Beakesbourne, Chartham, and Crundale, in the county of Kent, from* AD *1757 to* AD *1773*. London : Printed for the subscribers only

Fenwick, V. 1978. 'The Graveney boat: a tenth-century find from Kent'. British Archaeological Reports British Series 53

Frere, S.S. and Stow, S. 1983. 'Excavations in the St George's Street and Burgate Street Areas'. Canterbury: The Archaeology of Canterbury monograph series 7

Gaimster, M. 2005. 'Saxons in Deptford', *London Archaeologist*, 11 (2), 31–7

Gardiner, M., Cross, R., Macpherson-Grant, N. and Riddler, I. 2001. 'Continental trade
    and non-urban ports in mid-Saxon England: excavations at Sandtun, West Hythe, Kent',
    Archaeological Journal 158, 161–290

Hawkes, S.C. 2000. 'The Anglo-Saxon cemetery of Bifrons, in the parish of Patrixbourne, East
    Kent'. *Anglo-Saxon Studies in Archaeology and History* 11, 1–94

Hawkes, S.C. & Grainger, G. 2006. 'The Anglo-Saxon Cemetery at Finglesham, Kent'.
    Oxford: Oxford University School of Archaeology Monograph 64

Parfitt, K. and Brugmann, B. 1997. 'The Anglo-Saxon cemetery on Mill Hill, Deal, Kent'.
    Society for Mediaeval Archaeology Monograph 14, London

Perkins, D. 1991. 'The Jutish cemetery at Sarre revisited: a rescue evaluation'. *Archaeologia
    Cantiana* 109, 139–66

Philp, B. 1973. *Excavations in west Kent 1960–1970*. Dover: Kent Archaeological Rescue Unit

Philp, B. 2003. *The discovery and excavation of Anglo-Saxon Dover*. Dover: Kent Archaeological
    Rescue Unit

Roach Smith, C. 1871. *A catalogue of Anglo-Saxon and other antiquities discovered at Faversham*.
    London: Eyre and Spottiswode

Tyler, S. 1992. 'Anglo-Saxon settlement in the Darent valley and environs'. *Archaeologia
    Cantiana* 110, 71–81.

See also the journals *Archaeologia Cantiana*, *Kent Archaeological Review*, *Medieval Archaeology*,
Current Archaeology, *London Archaeologist* and *British Archaeology* for recently excavated sites.

General texts about Anglo-Saxon and Viking Age England

Arnold, C. 1982. *The Anglo-Saxon Cemeteries of the Isle of Wight*. London: British Museum

Attenborough, F. (ed.) 1922. *The Laws of the Earliest English Kings*. Cambridge: University Press

Bassett, S. (ed.) 1989. *The Origins of the Anglo-Saxon Kingdoms*. Leicester: Leicester University
    Press

Bede, The Venerable. *Ecclesiastical history of the English People*. London: Penguin

Blair, J. 2000. *The Anglo-Saxon age: a very short introduction*. Oxford: Oxford University Press

Blair, J. 2005. *The Church in Anglo-Saxon Society*. Oxford: Oxford University Press

Campbell, J. (ed.). 1991. *The Anglo-Saxons*. London: Penguin.

Charles-Edwards, T. 2003. *After Rome, Short Oxford History of British Isles*. Oxford: Oxford
    University Press

Davies, W. 2003. *From the Vikings to the Normans, Short Oxford History of the British Isles*.
    Oxford: Oxford University Press

Fell, C. 1986. *Women in Anglo-Saxon England*. Oxford: Blackwell

Garmondsway, G.N. (trans.) 1976. *The Anglo-Saxon Chronicle*. London: Dent

Gelling, M. 1997 3rd Ed. *Signposts to the past: place-names and the history of England*.
    Chichester: Phillimore

Gelling, M. 1984. *Place-names in the Landscape.* London: Dent

Hall, R. 1990. *Viking Age Archaeology in Britain and Ireland.* Princes Risborough: Shire Books

Hamerow, H. 2002 *Early Medieval Settlements*, Oxford: Oxford University Press

Haslam, J. (ed.). 1984. *Anglo-Saxon Towns in Southern England.* Chichester: Philimore

Hill, D. 1981. *An Atlas of Anglo-Saxon England.* London: Blackwell

Hindley, G. 2006. *A brief history of the Anglo-Saxons.* London: Constable and Robinson

Hinton, D. 1990, *Archaeology, Economy and Society.* London: Seaby

Hinton, D. A. 2005. *Gold and gilt, pots and pins: possessions and people in medieval Britain.* Oxford: University Press

Hodges, R. 1989. *The Anglo-Saxon Achievement.* London: Duckworth.

Lapidge, M. *et al* (eds). 2001. *The Blackwell Encyclopedia of Anglo-Saxon England.* Oxford: Blackwell

Leahy, K. 2003. *Anglo-Saxon crafts.* Stroud: Tempus

Lucy, S. 2000. *The Anglo-Saxon way of Death.* Stroud: Sutton

Mayr-Harting, H. 1991. *The Coming of Christianity to Anglo-Saxon England.* London: Batsford

Meaney, A. 1964. *A gazetteer of Anglo-Saxon burial sites.* London: Allen and Unwin

Morris, R. 1989. *Churches in the Landscape.* London: Dent

Ottaway, P. 1992, *Archaeology in British Towns from Emperor Claudius to the Black Death.* London: Routledge

Owen-Crocker, G. 2004. *Dress in Anglo-Saxon England.* Woodbridge: The Boydell Press

Reynolds, A. 1999. *Later Anglo-Saxon England, Life and Landscape.* Stroud: Tempus

Richards, J.D. 1991. *Viking Age England.* London: Batsford

Roesdahl, E. 1991. *The Vikings.* London: Penguin

Rogers, P.W. 2007. *Cloth and clothing in early Anglo-Saxon England* AD *450–700.* York: Council for British Archaeology

Sawyer, P.H. 1997 *The Oxford Illustrated History of the Vikings.* Oxford: Oxford University Press

Stenton, F. 1943. (2001 paperback edition) *Anglo-Saxon England.* Oxford: Oxford University Press

Taylor, H.M. 1978. *Anglo-Saxon Architecture Vol III.* Cambridge: Cambridge University Press

Taylor, H.M. and Taylor, J. 1965. *Anglo-Saxon Architecture Vols I and II.* Cambridge: Cambridge University Press

Underwood, R. 1999. *Anglo-Saxon weapons and warfare.* Stroud: Tempus

Webster, L. and Backhouse, J. 1991 *The Making of England: Anglo-Saxon art and culture* AD *600–900.* London: British Museum

Welch, M. 1992. *Anglo-Saxon England.* London: English Heritage

Wilson, D.M. (ed.).1976. *The Archaeology of Anglo-Saxon England.* London: Methuen

Wilson, D.M. 1984. *Anglo-Saxon Art.* London: Thames and Hudson

Wood, I. 1992. 'Frankish hegemony in England'. In Carver, M. (ed.) *The Age of Sutton Hoo*, 235-41. Woodbridge: Boydell Press

Yorke, B. 1997. *Kings and Kingdoms in early Anglo-Saxon England*. London: Routledge

Anglo-Saxon Kentish artefact studies

Ager, B.M. 1989. 'An Anglo-Saxon supporting-arm brooch from Eastry, Kent', *Medieval Archaeology* 33, 48–151

Brookes, S. 2007. 'Boat-rivets in graves in pre-Viking Kent: reassessing Anglo-Saxon boat-burial traditions'. *Medieval Archaeology* 51, 1–18

Evison, V. 1967. 'The Dover ring-sword and other sword-rings and beads', *Archaeologia* 101, 63–118

Leigh, D. 1984. 'The Kentish keystone-garnet disc brooches: Avent's classes 1–3 reconsidered'. *Anglo-Saxon Studies in Archaeology and History* 3, 67–76

Web resources

http://www.ads.ahds.ac.uk – Archaeological Data Service: the best and most comprehensive online catalogue, online archives and resources, including the forthcoming Early Anglo-Saxon Census that has a full listing of burials in Kent and associated artefacts

http://www.pastscape.org.uk – An excellent online archive drawing on information held by the National Monuments Record. Fully searchable for thumbnail sketches of sites, maps and references

http://www.pase.ac.uk/ – The Prosopography of Anglo-Saxon England is a listing of all of the inhabitants of England from the late sixth to the end of the eleventh century, recorded in written sources

http://www-cm.fitzmuseum.cam.ac.uk/emc/ – The Corpus of Early Medieval coin finds lists all single coin finds in the British Isles from AD 410–1180.

http://www.finds.org.uk/ – The website of the Portable Antiquities Scheme, with a searchable database of metal-detected finds

INDEX OF PEOPLE
AND PLACES

Page numbers in *italic* indicate illustrations